PO_

to

POET

POET
to
POET

CONTEMPORARY
WOMEN POETS
FROM JAPAN

edited by
Rina Kikuchi &
Jen Crawford

RECENT
WORK
PRESS

Poet to Poet
Recent Work Press
Canberra, Australia

National Library of Australia
Cataloguing-in-Publication entry is available at
http://catalogue.nla.gov.au

ISBN: 9780648087854(paperback)

Cover illustration: © Rikuzentakata City Museum, 1990
The cover image is a photo taken from *Catalogue: Oshirasama-dolls in
Rikuzentakata (Zuroku: Rikuzentakata no Oshirasama,* March 1990, published
by Rikuzentakata City Museum). It shows oshirasama dolls from the
Rikuzentakata City Museum collection. We are grateful to the Museum
for permission to use this image.

We would like to pay our respects to the staff of the Rikuzentakata
City Museum who lost their lives in the 2011 earthquake and tsunami
disaster, and to those who survive them. We would like to offer special
appreciation to Masaru Kumagai, a chief curator, who has since the disaster
worked to restore the Museum and its collections under the most difficult
circumstances.

This book project was supported by the Japanese government's KAKEHNI
research grant, 15KK0049.

Cover design: Recent Work Press
Set by Recent Work Press

recentworkpress.com

Contents

Introduction

This book is the outcome of a translation project formed around the idea of poets translating poets. It was conceived last December, in the middle of the Australian summer, at my first meeting with New Zealand/Australian poet, Jen Crawford. The book was planned as an accompaniment to a Japanese women's bilingual poetry reading at the Poetry on the Move Festival (September 2017) at the University of Canberra, which would feature the works of four invited women poets. However, the project expanded as we included other Australian-based poets in the translation process. It soon became an anthology of ten Japanese women poets, carefully matched with poet/translators according to the particular character of the poetics of each. Accordingly, this book is not intended as a comprehensive representation of Japanese women poets writing today. Rather, it is a celebration of work that allowed us to weave a dynamic conversation across hemispheres.

The aim of this project has been to translate or transform poems originally written in Japanese into poems that live and breathe as poems in English. As the only native Japanese speaker on the translating side of this project, I tried to bridge poets who write in Japanese and poets who write in English, often becoming a messenger between the poets in order to support the translation process.

In the course of this work, I often questioned what it was I was trying to translate. Poetry is an artform made in language. Yet paradoxically, what I was translating was often not the words. With each of my poet co-translators, I spent hours discussing and explaining the layers of the meaning behind individual words or phrases, in what situations a word can be used, the effects of sounds and strange word-orders, images evoked by the lines, the usage of space, superscripts and other types of Japanese script. Through these discussions, I came to realise what we were trying to translate was not what was written on the page, but rather, what was not written. The goal of translation then for me became to re-create in English what one sees and feels when one reads the original poem in Japanese.

I had to struggle with a dilemma whenever a beautiful poem in English of its own right was born through our co-translation process. How close and faithful should a translation be? Following the work of our vigorous discussions, I decided to respect my co-translators' decisions about word-order or lineage. Some of the translations use lineage, tense, and word orders in ways that are apparently not equivalent to the original. Some words of the source poem may not be directly represented, and words with no direct equivalents may be added. In each case I believe these changes help the reader of the poem in English to see and feel what's carried by the original poem.

It is often asked if poetry translations 'lose' something of their originals. Maybe they do. However, I argue that they gain, too. Good examples are the puns that emerge in the translations of 'Dollogy' and 'Soles'. In 'Dollogy', the word 'mummy' means not only the bodies of the girls who were sacrificed, but also suggests the long history of mother-daughter relationships and what is passed from women to women through those relationships, which is so much a part of this poem's unspoken content. The pun is not in the original. In the same way, the poem 'Soles' in English talks about the sole fish as in the Japanese original, but at the same time, suggests the lost 'souls' of human beings who become 'soles' and the 'soles of the shoes'.

The translation process and approach was different with each co-translator, but we sat together and read original poems together, talked about the poet each translator was dealing with, talked through the poems line by line. We kept meeting and discussing, and went through the revisions many times. During the process, I also asked questions of the Japanese poets. The act of translation became a way of communicating between the poets in two different languages through poetry.

The responsibility for the selection of the poets and poems here lies with me. I have chosen to focus on women, firstly because I believe modern and contemporary women poets in Japan remain overlooked in the male-dominant Japanese literary canon (chosen by the male-dominant Japanese literary academia) despite claims that this is no longer true in the 21st century. Secondly, images of Japanese women in English-speaking countries have been doubly filtered by orientalism and sexism, thus outdated stereotypes of their 'obedient' and 'passive' nature need to be displaced and discarded. In order to make this anthology an illusion-breaker, I have chosen the poets and poems not to present a collective image of 'contemporary Japanese women' but to demonstrate a variety and diversity of women's voices. I have included poets of all ages, award-winning and emerging, Tokyo-based and members of the diaspora, activists, business-women and women who work in the home. The poems are variously satirical, humorous, cynical, playful, political, heart-wrenching, heart-warming, historical, mythological, philosophical, surreal and/or realistic.

Informed by many discussions, we have chosen to print the texts of the Japanese poems vertically, next to their English translations, so that the reader can see the poems in both languages together. With this decision we aimed to make visible the close conversation between languages and poets that is fundamental to this project. Bilingual editions of Japanese and English create difficult layout decisions, because of the conflict between two different reading traditions: one horizontal and left-to-right, and the other vertical, right-to-left. No solution is perfect, but we feel that the awkwardness generated here by inverted page-turns for readers of the Japanese poems reflects something of the act of translation itself. Translation crosses boundaries, disrupts comforts and brings the strangeness and newness of an encounter with another culture. By presenting this awkwardness on the page we hope we are sharing with all of our readers the joy of that freshness, as well as its disruption.

I thank all the poets, Jen Crawford, Niloofar Fanaiyan, Subhash Jaireth, Paul Munden, Shane Strange, who were brave enough to become part of this project and translate Japanese poems into English without knowing a word of Japanese. Some might call this foolhardy, but the richness of the conversations that it required speaks through the translations themselves. Thank you, Cassandra Atherton and Melinda Smith, whose knowledge of Japanese literature and language added another layer of richness. I thank Carol Hayes, a passionate scholar of Japanese poetry, who has been my long-time co-translator.

The exception to our translation process for this volume has been the work of the eminent poet Ito Hiromi, one of the Poetry on the Move Festival guests. Ito Hiromi's poetry is widely available in translation, and we were fortunate to be able to use existing translations by Jeffrey Angles. I thank publisher Michael Brennan of Vagabond Press, for his kind permission in allowing us to do this.

I thank all the Japanese poets for not only giving permission for translation, but for kindly answering all my never-ending questions, checking old diaries and materials in order to elaborate on the poems and their backgrounds, talking on the phone or in person for hours and hours, and writing lengthy emails back and forth with me. I could not have finished this book without their encouragement.

I am grateful to Shane Strange, publisher and editor at Recent Work Press for his courage and effort in taking on the complex challenge of a bilingual poetry text. I am also grateful to Chisa Nishino, a research assistant at Shiga University, Japan, for her support in this translation project.

Special thanks for Jen Crawford, who started this project with me, and from the start to the last, worked towards the ideal that all that is in the original poems could be there in our translations.

Rina Kikuchi
Canberra, August 2017

ARAI TAKAKO
新井高子

translated by

JEN CRAWFORD
ジェン・クロフォード
&
RINA KIKUCHI
菊地利奈

電球

だァらりと、お低頭バしながら咲いとっだよ、一重咲ぎの寒椿が。生垣のその一輪、しゃっくって見や

れば、戸口から、年増女が口紅ひいて、「電球、お助けくださいませんか」。

ひょっと、合点しぢまったァのす、土地ことばじゃねえもんで。上がりッ端サ脱ぐボロ靴、恥ずかし

かっだなや。「あのひとと同じ靴下」、妙に通ったその声が、こっちの背すじサ、ひゃッと走って。

軋んだっけえ、床板も。

馬鹿に高げえ杉天井。おらの背丈でも届かしねぇ。指され、納戸の脚立バ探して戻りゃァ、

立っでごぜんす、

大年増が

綸子の緋色の襦袢姿で。

障子越しの薄ッすら明がりに、うづ向いておりやした、伊達締めバ弄りくさって。脱ぎすてたメリン

スの袂バ踏むのは、もう素足や（こりゃ、気狂げえだイ）。脚立バうッ捨り、踵を返えしたのは言う

2　新井高子

A Lightbulb

Withered while bowing, tsubaki—single bloom on the hedge. Scoop it up & there's—this old girl, lipsticked, watching from a doorway: 'A lightbulb. Perhaps you could help?'

It startles me, her stranger's phrasing. Yes. Better go in, better shed these worn-out scuffs. 'The same socks as him!' Her voice runs clear & cold down my back. The floor creaks—

Her ceiling's unbelievably high. Can't reach it—not me. She points, I go for the stepladder, come back,

& she's standing—

this old girl

in her bright red wrap

In dim light through paper screen I can see her looking down, touching her sash, her sleeves, standing on the kimono's fallen layers— feet bare already! Crazy! I drop the ladder, of course, & turn to go—

'Pardon me. I'm not going to do anything. I just want you to take a look.' Her voice is pleading, catching me. Thin, thinner, sharpening, red, the whet barb hooking my ear's depth. Ahh—ahh—her breath pushes back, her scent's rising like smoke, my heart chokes, I turn—we turn to one another. Her make-up's slipping. I can see her naked face.

Ogres, snakes—I'll take what I can get. Pull it together, go to her. Push her down, tear open the wrap—what? Another underneath— silk, fine and white as a shroud. 'I told you, I just want you to take a look.' Her thighs are twisting, she's wrapping herself back up. Her

までもねェがす。

「もぉし、なんにもいたしません。見ていただきたいだけなのです」、追いすがるその声が、オッ放してくれんがよ。かぼそい声尻、なお研いで、尖らして、真っ赤な針バおらの耳根サ引ッ掛けで、ハァ、ハァ、ハァ、ハァ、荒がってぐ女の息が、煙り立ってぐその匂いが、胸苦しゅうで振り向かざるを得んのした。瞳が合うと、ひゅうッと澄んだよ、流れた化粧の下の素顔が。

鬼でも蛇でも来ィやがれェ。覚悟して、ツッ倒し、ヒッ裂ぎりゃア、着込んでおるがや、もう一皮。

「見ていただきたいだけなんです」、羽二重のその白襦袢が、内股よじって、裾お直しゃる。経帷子にも見えだっけェ。まるで臨終し立てのごとく、額の皺がサッと退ぎ、お蠟のように涼しい顔に、カッと灯った真深き瞳。おらは夢中で衿ヒッつかみ、開かす片胸、ざぐらッと。

ごせぇませんのした、

乳房は。

み雪のように平らがで、一匹の五寸百足が、「手術して二十年です」。

face smooths, cool & waxy, her eyes flash a deep red. I grab the neck,
pull at it, grab her breast—

it's not there

her breast

a handspan cut

smooth as mountain snow

& Scolopendra flat.

'The operation was twenty years ago.'

★

the operation   twenty years   ahh   like this   you've
    looked down on me the sea of my breast surging   reviving
    ahh   so red   the scar that tips my heart

    reviving   as if new-born   ridges swelling, yes?   Scorpius
    of my breast

    ahh   these stitches   the scissors

like the tail, yes?   the needle-tip puncturing

and should I let this stretch   *ahh*   *ahh*   with my
    deepest breath?

＊

手術して、二十年です。ハァ、ハァ、ハァ、ハァ、こうしてあなたに見下ろされ、胸の海が波立つ

と、吹き返してきますでしょう、ハァ、ハァ、ハァ、ハァ、赤々と、心の臓の真上の傷が。たった

いま、生まれたように腫れ上がってきたでしょう。蠍ですよ、わたしの胸の。ハァ、ハァ、鋏だも

の、ここの縫い目が。抉った深傷の針さきは、まるでお星座の尻尾でしょう。伸び上がらしてみま

しょうか、こうして息を膨らして。ハァ、ハァ、ハァ、ハァ。

あの朝、椿が咲きました、病院の生垣に一輪だけ。

わたしは白い浴衣を着せられ、鼻すじがあなたによく似た医者でした。

麻酔が効いて、モヤのなかの迷子の耳にも、声は響いて「はじめます」、

恐くて、目の裏、こじ開けました、

カッと灯ったその電球、焼き付いたままなのです、わたしの奈落の水鏡に。

はやく点けてくださいまし、もういちど、

6　　新井高子

That morning a bloom   single, on the hospital hedge.

I was put in a white gown. The doctor looked like you, with your
   strong nose.

The anaesthetic began to work

                              and through the haze to my lost ears

the voice echoed

                         Let's begin

frantic   I prised open   my inner lids

          & the bulb's sting   was printed

          on the water mirror

                              my inner abyss

Quickly, turn it on   again

you look like him   today again

                              the hedge

                         and in a white gown

               I   bloom   yes

あなたはよく似た医者で、きょうも、わたしは白いきもので

咲いたでしょう、生垣だって

点けて、ほら、

掠ったよ、掠ったもの、あなたの鋏はひゃっこいねぇ、

もっともっと波打って、見せますから、熱い赤ァい鋏を、わたしは

ずっとずっと白いきもので、あなたはずっと医者さまで、

切ったでしょう、白い椿を、

散切りにしたでしょう、だから赤いきもので出たんじゃないか！

どうして点かないのさ！、電球だけが、

こじ開けたんだよ、毒針が、ヒッ掻いたんだよ、目蓋とあたしを、

ツッ刺して、オッ被さって、

カッと、灯しゃアいいだろう

8　新井高子

Turn it on   c'mon

you just brush past me   with your scissors   so chilly
and I'm surging   surging   showing   hot red scissors
I   forever   and ever in a white gown
you   forever the doctor

slashed them, didn't you?   the white tsubaki
chopped them into pieces   so I came in red!

Why doesn't it turn on!
                    the single bulb
the poisoned needle   prising
                                scratching   at my eyelids
scratching me stabbing   pushing me down   stinging bright

Just turn it on!

                    so sweet, this anaesthetic haze.

                                                so chilly
I'll puff puff till I burst
swell

麻酔のモヤって美味しいねぇ、こんなにも涼しいもの、はち切れたって吸うんだ、あたしは、

どんどんどんどん脹れて脹れて、このお腹、気持ち悪りィかい？

吊るっとくれよ、生垣に

赤でも白でも開くんだから、花なんて

風に吹かれる電球だろ、あたしが、

花提灯だよ、すっぱい夜露のお星さまだよ

よじのぼって、この縫い糸を歯に喰い縛って、よじのぼって、

宙吊りで、宙ぶらりんで、雁字搦めのしたたる蠍が、腹ぼての大蠍が、

映るよ、

この姫鏡に

電球、電球、電球点けろ！

and swell

      my belly

            gross, yes?

         don't

let me hang on the hedge.

Red or white, it doesn't matter.

   it blooms anyway—

     the flower

        lightbulb swinging in the wind

          I

      pendant   star of the sour night dew

clambering, stitched thread clenching clambering

hanging, dangling, Scorpius, bound up, springing droplets

   swollen   scorpion belly

reflecting   in this image, this compact

   lightbulb, a lightbulb, a lightbulb

    Turn it on

おーしらさま考

まっさか膨れでおらっしゃるなぁ。ぎゅう、ぎゅッと、細帯締めで。

春ァ来るたび、赤い衣ッコ欲しがるがら、着膨れ上がってしまわれだったァ、おーしらさまは。裾めぐりゃァ、臭うがや。煮染めだみだいに、ショボ垂れだ何枚も、何枚も。

肉だよ、そりゃァ。毎年毎年、新らし布ッコおっ被りゃァ、熟らすがや、中身のそれァ。ぎょうさん黴だちゃ飼っとるだっぎゃァ。春サ来で、蠢めぇとるぎゃァ、ほろほろほろ。

なァに、蚕の唾汁だもの、肉汁だァもの、臭うがよ、絹糸は。製糸工場サ行ったこだァねぇのすか。鼻ッぽ火ィ付ぐどぉ、繭玉は、皮だもの、生皮だァもの。湿気で腐りゃァ、還えるンべぇや、肉塊サ。

おーしらさまは、木乃伊でおらしゃるがぁ、お蚕の、
おーしらさまは、木乃伊でおらしゃるがぁ、娘ッコの。

昔なァ、おったづなァ、おーしらさまの心棒みだいな娘っこが。ダゲーン、ダゲーン、木割で両腕ブッ斬らィ、立っとっとだァ。人柱アさね。人の柱バお手向げするづよ、山神に。お返えしだァもの、ぎょうさんの木柱の。

立っとっとだァ、あの娘ゃァ、止まンにゃァもの、肩の血ィ。月の血が。ぎゅう、ぎゅッと、杙サ縛らィ、飛沫イだっぎゃァ、胎がらも。

Dollogy

Oh! You're even rounder than I expected. Cinched in by a skinny belt.

Every spring you need a new red dress, so now you're fat with layers, a bundled-up ball. Girl-doll. What a stink when your hem's picked up—as if those layers were stewed in soy for days. Layers, layers fraying, then more layers.

Fresh layers every year. You put on new ones as the ones inside mature. And there inside you tend your many moulds. In spring they wriggle, teem, and like blossoms fall away.

Well, it all makes sense—the silk threads are both the spit of the worms and their boiled-up flesh, so of course they stink. You've been to the silk mill, right? The stench burns your nostrils because the cocoons are peeled skin. And so these layers, rotten with damp, turn back to flesh.

Of course. Girl-dolls are the mummies of silk worms.

Of course. Girl-dolls are the mummies of young girls.

Once there was a girl like a girl-doll pole—whack, whack!—standing, with arms chopped off. Human sacrifice, yes? The human pole offered to the mountain goddess. We give thanks for all the lumber we're given, of course!

Standing, she can't stop the flow of blood from her shoulders. Moon-blood. She's cinched to the pole and it splashes, even from her womb.

And can't stop, even after her last breath is gone,

止まンねにゃァ、息サ絶ィでも、
　　ヒン剝がィでも、山神に、生皮バ。

おーしらさまは、身代ァりどぉ、あんだァの、
　　おーしらさまは、身代ァりどぉ、山神さァまの。

春ァ来るたび、若げぇ皮ッコ欲しがるがら、膨れ上がってしまわれだったァ、孕レンみだいに肥えだ
ったァ、山神さァまは。祝っだなァ、息ンだなァ。新らし花ッコ、山陰がら何本も、何本も。

何百も、何千も、

年バ重ねで、

拵せぇでけろ、おらァの遺骸お。ゆっぐら、ゆっぐら、着しでけろ、お蚕の肌コぉ。
赤いの、けらい。
染みっぢまァもの、止まンにゃァもの。裾めぐりゃァ、臭うべや。

月だよ、
そりゃァ。

14　　新井高子

even after the goddess has stripped her skin.

Girl-doll is standing in for you.

Girl-doll is standing in for the mountain goddess.

Every spring you need new skin, so now you're plump with life.
Goddess.

Celebrating the breath-push. Blossoms, then more blossoms from
within your mountain gorge. For hundreds of years, thousands of years

layering age—

Please, please make a corpse for me, slowly, slowly put the skins on

give me red ones

*because I'll dye them, because I can't stop. Of course it stinks when you lift
these layers.*

That's

the moon.

機神考

ぎゅんぎゅんぎゅんぎゅん、　駆けずっておりました
機屋のまわりを
神さまが、
素ッ裸の神さまが、　犬歯を垂らし、

布を織る
あるいは買う、
わたしたちは生産する、　消費する、　消耗する
いいえ、
もっと根源で
消えたもの、
　　　消されたもの

裸ンぼうで歩くのを止めただろう、　わたしたちは
獣の皮を纏って
その頭を祀るのも、　歌って踊るのも、

Mechanimism

crankrankrankrankrank

around the silk mill runs

a god,

stark naked, canines looming—

    whether we weave the material

    or buy it

    we produce, consume, expend—

    no—

    there's something deeper:

    what's vanished,

        what was made to vanish—

    we stopped walking naked, yes?

    put on the animal's skin

    & sang, danced, worshipped its severed head,

    the material woven,

    the roots of the downy hair

繊維の
うぶ毛の根ッコは
臭う、
葬られたものたちの息

ぎゅんぎゅんぎゅんぎゅん、　駆けずっておりました
機屋のまわりを
四つ足で、
毛むくじゃらで、　むんむん曲がった鼻づらが、

喰らッちまったがですよ
べろらッと、
織り子らを
糸を吐きだす女らを、

「おもてへ出ろィ！」

reeking

with the breath of what's buried—

crankrankrankrankrank

around the silk mill

on four legs,

furry, sticky, horny-nosed,

it gobbles up

gulp!

the mill women

who spit the thread—

get out of here!

ARAI TAKAKO
新井高子

translated by

CAROL HAYES
キャロル・ヘイズ
&
RINA KIKUCHI
菊地利奈

フレアスカート

　あたしが、

　ありゃア、

女学校サあがる春休みのことで。飼い猫のブチが、子バ産みまして、一匹だけ。ハァ年増でしたんで、きりきり精バしぼったッとでしょう、げっそりと、刃物みてぇに険バ立て、チィーミャア、チィーミャア、二十日鼠のようなのが甘がる懐ころサ、必死に隠しておりやした。独り身が、不義の子こせぇたようでした。

しばらく前、初潮バありました、あたしに。夕暮れの新聞屋に集金わたす縁側で、ひょっと、染まっておったんです、フレアスカートが。翌日、母さんは、ぼうぼう二升も赤飯炊いて、

「お嬢、とうとう仲間入りかィ」

織り子のカッちゃんは、物干し竿のスカートめくり、

「いまの流行りだがよぉ」

ミサちゃんは、桃色のパンティーさし出し、

機械なおしのシモやんたら、

あたしの尻バ軍手でこすり、「上玉、上玉！」

新聞記事じゃねぇがよ、メンスは、

おっ母ちゃん！

Flared Skirt

It was...

I was...

It was the spring holidays just before I started girls' high. Our tabby cat Buchi had kittens, only one though. But then she was very old. She twisted it out using up all her strength, wearing herself out, furious like the edge of a knife, eeeek-mew eeeek-mew, the tiny mouse-like creature snuggled tight against her breast, as she tried desperately to hide the little one from view. Like an unwed mother birthing a bastard child.

A while ago, that first bleeding happened, to me. On the narrow back deck where we handed over the money to the newspaper boy in the evenings, suddenly, stained, my flared skirt. The next day, mother cooked up twenty cups of celebratory red bean rice:

'Miss, you're finally one of us women'

says Kat-chan, one of the weaving girls, pulling up the skirt on the clothesline to expose the inside,

'They're the latest fashion'

says Misa-chan, giving me some peach-coloured panties,

and Shimo-yan, who fixes the looms, strokes my bottom with his work-gloved hands, 'so round, so plump'

ブチは、そもそも野良猫でした。いえ、その時分は、生ッ粋の家猫なんぞおりゃアせん。軒下の残飯あさり、むっくり炬燵サもぐりッ込むずうずうしさで。ギャッとすり抜かる。鼻ふくらしソッポする。抱いたことなぞねぇがすよ。

辛かったね、あたしは辛かった。煙草くせぇシモやんに、尻撫でらィた瞬間に、ずるっと垂れた経血が。ミサちゃんとお揃いのパンティー穿いて、街場サ行ぐかと想うのも。三時休みの赤飯に、エ場の前歯が、ズラッとオッ立ち、きゅうッと鳴ったよ、あたしのがらんどうは。カッちゃんの下ッ腹イは、二十日鼠が埋まってるって。六ケ月だッてがァ。

松飾りがとれた晩だった。

捨てッ子かィ、

また、女工が

あんまし切ない大泣きサしたもんで、中庭から。半纏ひっかけ、生け垣の根もとバ見りゃア、おったんよ、あのブチが。霜サ蕩かす声あげて、擦すりッ付けてた、地べたに腹を。

オギャうあアーン、

横ゾッポーがオッ被さると、ぎりぎり尾っぽバ持ち上げて、ケツつき出す姥桜。果てると、ギャアッと勝ち気がもどり、

追っ払ったよ、隣りんちのオス猫バ。

It's not a newspaper story! My period!

Mummm!

Buchi was originally a stray. But then, at that time there were no pure house cats. Scrounging for food scraps under the eaves, slyly crawling in under the kotatsu table, she's absolutely shameless. When I try to stroke her back she slips past me with a hiss. She snorts and turns away. I never manage to get my arms round her.

It was hard wasn't it? It was for me. When Shimo-yan, with his tobacco stink, stroked my bottom, my blood oozed out in a slimy slurp. An' then thinking about having to go out into town wearing the same panties as Misa-chan. And then at the three o'clock break, when the front teeth of the factory workers lined up for the red bean rice, my inner void clenched in emptiness. They're saying somebody's buried a house mouse in Kat-chan's lower belly. Six months already.

It was the night when we took down the New Year pine decorations.

Huh? An abandoned child?

It's a factory girl again.

The crying was so heart wrenching, coming from the factory yard. I pulled on my hanten jacket to look around near the base of the fence, and there she was. That Buchi. Yowling with a cry that would melt frost, rubbing her belly along the ground.

Waaah-meiooooowww

As the tomcat starts to ride her, the cougar forces up her tail and sticks out her arse. After the deed is done, —raaww—her unyielding

跡とり娘です、一人ッ子です、あたしも。

女学校でて婿さんもらって機屋サ継いで、カッちゃん、ミサちゃんの給金つづかし、その子まで、そ

の姑まで。

あたしの婚交（くながい）が、喰わスンですよ、

　　　月のしずくが

　　　喰わすがですよ、

　　　工場の鼠を

　　　　　みなの衆、おめでとさんでござります

　　　　昇ってきょッたぞ

　　　　　　　あたくし奴（め）に、

　　　どす赤い新月が

　　心臓みてぇにぶるぶる震え、

　　輝いて

　　したたったよ

　　つつつーーーッと、

　　ホンモンの　赤けぇゴハンぞ

　　ほれ、

　　シモやん、すべって溺れるなィ

　　ようカッちゃん、うンめぇかい

willfulness returns and she drives him off, that male cat from next door.

The daughter and heir, the only child, I'm the same.

I'll finish girl's high, get a husband, inherit the factory, continue to pay Kat-chan and Misa-chan, their children, and even their mothers-in-law. My marital intercourse will feed them.

It's my monthlies—my moon drops

That feed them!

The factory house mice

All of you—congratulations!

It's rising up

In me

The blood red new moon

Quivering like a trembling heart

Shining

Dripping

A sticky ……. trail of drops

This is it   genuine red rice!

Look at it!

Shimo-yan! Don't slip and drown.

Hey, Kat-chan. Tasty isn't it.

Newspaper man! Come on, go ahead

新聞屋さん、ご遠慮のう　お撮りなさんし
フレアスカートの中の　破顔と厚顔は、
無礼講にござりますとも！

翌朝、おっ母ちゃんが雨戸サ開けると染まってる、仏間の畳が。ブチがおる。うら暗れぇ眼でこっち
バ見上げ、口サぬったり汚しッつかし。
喰らってしまったがですよ、可愛いかわいい二十日鼠バ、自分の八重歯でブッ刺して。

なりとうなかよぉ

　　　　　　女に、

けぇりたがよぉ

母ちゃんサお腹の

　　　　　　　　鼠に、あたしも

のう、ブチや、

搾れんかったか

おめぇの痩したその乳にゃァ

白れぇゴハンさ　出されんかったか

泣くるあたしを横目に猫は、ほどなく工場サ出てゆきました。

> take as many photos as you like

My smiling my shamelessness
> inside my flared skirt

Don't stand on ceremony! Go for it!

The next morning, when mum opened the shutters—it was stained. The tatami, where we had the altar to the family dead. There was Buchi. She looked up at us with dark shadowed eyes, her mouth thick with a filthy wetness.

She'd eaten it. Her own lovely sweet little house mouse. Impaled on her canines.

I don't want to be
> A woman,

I want to go back

As the mouse
> In mum's belly, me too

Hey, Buchi,

Couldn't you squeeze anything out

Of those bony breasts

No one fed you any did they?　　　Any white rice?

With only a sidelong glance, ignoring me crying, the cat soon left the factory.

ヘルド

機械と女の喧噪が、夕ぐれへ吸い込まれても、
糸置き場におりました、あたしは
束に寄っかかると、首の痏えがおりました
鉱泉のにおいがします、絹が吐き出す夜気というのは、
幻燈です
ひとつだけ、電球が灯ってて
板戸の穴から覗く、工場のありようは、
幻燈です

冷たい指が
織り機のヘルドに触れようとしています
機の止まった夜にこそ、現れるのです、男は
経糸の繫ぎ屋です
乾いたすきま風と、
フィラメントに、晃々としていくヘルドの、
ちいさな、ちいさな目の中へ
挿し込もうとしています、糸を

The Healds

The clatter and chatter of the looms and the women had faded into
    the dusk,

There I was, still in the thread storeroom

Leaning on the spools of thread, the stiffness in my neck disappeared

A tang of sulphur, the night air the silk spits out

Is a magic lantern

Alone, a single bulb glows

Peering through the hole in the wooden door, the factory

Is a magic lantern

Cold fingers

About to touch the healds of the loom

Just at night, when the looms are at rest, he appears, the man

The warp threader

About to push through, the thread

Into the healds, glittering in a draft of dry wind

Under the filament of the bulb

Into their tiny, tiny eyes

Forbidden to blink

瞬きのゆるされない

空ろの目、

織機とは

手というまえに

無数の、無名の、瞳の変身ですから、

糸の交差を、すみずみまで見届けるのは

そんな眼球たちですから、

ぶら下がるヘルドは、義眼と言ってもいいんです、女工さんの、

夜の男は

一本、一本

しらっと舐めあげ

突き通さねばなりません、

痛がるでしょう

男の背中も、あんなに震えていて、

眉をひそめたヘルドは

ほうり投げるでしょう、視線を、

格子窓の新月へ

Vacant eyes,

Because the looms

Before they are hands

Are the transformations of numberless, nameless eyes

Because they're the sort of eyeballs that

Watch every single threaded intersection

The hanging healds can be called the artificial eyes of the factory girls

The night man

First one, then the next

Lightly moistening each with his tongue

Must push it through

It will hurt

The man's back too is trembling hard

Grimacing, the healds

Will look away

Through the window grating towards the new moon

Are the looms

Perhaps marionettes? At this textile factory

If they don't let it in they can't work

If they let it in, they can get moving eyes, the healds

機械とは、
操つり人形かもしれませんね、織物工場では
通さなければ、はたらけないのです
通されれば、うごく瞳が持てるんです、ヘルドは
男へ
カタッと、
首の関節を折り
蒼い息を吹きかけます、その針に
滲む、
ルビーの血色こそ、視力です

一体、一体、吊るされて
天井から、
しのびこむ鎌いたちに
糸と、
糸が、
絡まると
ばんざいする、蹴り足する、
乗りだして組みあう肩、腹をかかえて開ける下顎

With a clack

Fold their necks

Towards the man

Releasing a pale breath, along the needle

A spreading blur

This ruby red blood gives them vision

Hung up, one beside the other

From the ceiling,

The sneaking whirlwind catches

This thread

Then that

All entangled

Arms lift in banzai, legs kicking

Leaning forwards, embracing shoulders, holding bellies, laughing jaws

The man

Races over, desperate to untangle them

Each demanding more attention

More more, penetrate me

Make me come!

Slyly exposing their breasts

男は、
駆けよって、解そうとヤッキになりますが、
かまわれたいのさ
もっともっと、突ッ込んでよ
いかしてよ、
胸もとがはだけていくのは
手管です、マリオネットの女工たちの、
眼ざしが
月へもどれば
頬に、ツツッとつたいます、
男のこめかみから滴ってくる汗が

今ごろ、
生身の女工さんらは
家や寄宿や銭湯で、
湯浴みをしている、娘の寝顔を見てる、電話の受話器をおこうとしている
いいえ、
いいえ、
梳しけずる

The feminine wiles　　　　of the marionette factory girls

When their coaxing gaze

Returns to the moon

Running down both cheeks

Sweat drips from the man's temples

Just about now

The real flesh and blood bodies of the factory girls

Taking their baths at home, boarding houses or public bathhouses
or watching the sleeping faces of their daughters, or just about to
hang up their phones

No,

No,

Combing their locks

Their rich hair, tangles in the wind

At precisely eleven o'clock

They try to force it through their hair, the comb

Is reflected in the mirror

Leaning forwards, embracing shoulders, holding bellies, laughing jaws

The marionettes are tangled in threads

The healds are

ゆたかな髪が、風にもつれる、

十一時かっきりに

挿し入れようとするはずです、櫛を

鏡にうつして、

乗り出して組みあう肩、腹をかかえて笑う下顎

糸まみれの人形です、

ヘルドは

いいえ、あたしたちは

操つられて、操つらして、操つって、

男がビームを回せば、

攣りあがります、

生えぎわが、毛穴ごと、

なんと気持ちの佳いことでしょう

丹念に

一条、一条、束ねては、

巻き上げます、男は

色とりどりのすじ糸を、あたしたちの毛髪を、

なんと艶めくことでしょう

No, we are

Being manipulated, allowing ourselves to be manipulated, manipulating him to manipulate us

As the man rolls up the warp beam

All pulled up

The roots of our hair, each and every hair follicle

How good does that feel!

Delicately

First one strand, then the next, weaving them together

Hoisting them up, the man works on

The multicoloured threads, our hair,

How alluring it looks!

The night factory, the night factory girls, the night coiffeur

All a magic lantern

The single light bulb

Like a pendulum

Swinging

Suddenly

Vanishes

With the warp threader

Before the echoing of the motor bike delivering the bottled milk

夜の工場に、夜の女工と、夜の髪結いさん

幻燈です

たったひとつの白熱球が、

振り子のように

揺すられて

サッと、

消える

繋ぎ屋といっしょに、

牛乳瓶を配達する、バイクの音がひびく前に

朝の光は、

人形を

機械に見してしまうでしょうが、

知ってるよ

男が置いてくつげ櫛を、

女工なら、

The morning light

Makes the marionettes

Look like looms

But you know

About that wooden comb the man leaves behind

If you're a factory girl, that is.

ISHIKAWA ITSUKO
石川逸子

translated by

PAUL MUNDEN
ポール・マンデン

&

RINA KIKUCHI
菊地利奈

ヒラメのこと

靴になれ
といわれたら　靴になった
おびただしい靴が　異国の橋を渡った

鋲になれ
といわれたら　鋲になった
だれを刺すためか　おびただしい鋲が道にあふれた

蜜柑になれ
といわれたら　蜜柑になった
売れ余った沢山の蜜柑が　掃いて捨てられた

椅子になれ
といわれたら　椅子になった
重たい尻に押しつぶされても　じっと黙って耐えた

Soles—

become shoes

on command: *become shoes!*

So many shoes—crossing the bridge to a foreign land...

hobnails

on command: *be hard as nails!*

Stab someone, anyone—nail the whole street...

become oranges

on command: *become oranges!*

So many oranges, unsold, going to waste—chucked out...

become chairs

on command: *become chairs!*

Hard pressed—we endure without muttering a word...

become frogs

on command: *become frogs!*

From spring through to summer—croak croak croak...

蛙になれ
といわれたら　蛙になった
長い夏の日を　啼いて過した

泥になれ
といわれたら　泥になった
泥になって　静かに蚊とんぼの歌をきいていた

といわれたら　脚立になった
脚立になれ
といわれたら　ブーメランになった
ブーメランになれ
といわれたら　葉っぱになった
葉っぱになれ

鷺と鷹にいっぺんになれ
といわれたら　体をちぎって鷺と鷹になった
けんかしろ

become mud

on command: *become mud!*

Mud—listening to the cranefly's summer song...

become a boomerang

on command: *boomerang!*

become a ladder

on command: *ladder!*

become leaves

on command: *leaves!*

become an eagle *and* a hawk

on command: *eagle! hawk!*

We tear our bodies in two

and *fight!*

on command: with airborn ferocity, clawing each other's eyes—

feeling each other's pain—from within...

with shredded skin—and while resting, bleeding,

we're commanded: *become a drum!*

Drum—such a sorrowful beat...

といわれたら　空中で烈しく眼を突つき合った
どちらも自分だったから　どちらがやられても痛かった

皮がむけ　血がにじんだ姿で休んでいたら
太鼓になれ　といわれた
太鼓になって　かなしい音で鳴った

こんどはネジになれ
といわれて苦しくネジになりそこなった太鼓は
つぶされ　火で焼かれた
ネジになった私たちは　じっと死んでゆく友を見た

人間にもどりたい
おびただしいネジがぶつぶつ云っていた
でも　ヒラメになれ　といわれると
やっぱりヒラメになった
しんからいやいやヒラメになったものは
ヒレがあっても泳げなかった

become a screw

we were told, but some struggled

and were crushed—burned...

our friends, dying under our riveted gaze.

Oh to return to our human form,

mumble the many screws,

only to become flat fish—on command

but they do it anyway, become soles...

and those soles who from the bottom of their hearts yearned to resist

gain fins but can't swim...

flailing—they float to the river's surface.

Others,

perfect transformations,

mock those adrift,

whose eyes are full of tears,

floundering, dying.

もがきながら　川の面に浮びあがる
いくつかのヒラメを
うまくヒラメになったものたちが
嘲笑って突ついた
眼に涙をためて
泳げないヒラメは死んでいった

それから長いこと
命令は下らなかった
ほんとうは人間で
ヒラメに化けただけのことを
靴になった日の苦しさや　蛙になった日のかなしみも
もう　ほとんどが忘れてしまった
いつか　人間にもどれる日がきたとき
ヒラメたちは　私たちは　どうするだろう

There follows an age

without command.

Human souls all along,

we just changed form:

painfully, into shoes; sorrowfully, into frogs;

all of that forgotten, by almost everyone.

Come the day—when we regain our humanity,

how will we cope, we poor soles?

狼・私たち

狼が口を血だらけにして兎を食べている
（円陣をつくって眺めている私たち）
狼はひどく腹が空いているのだ　あわれな眼附きをした兎の顔を
彼は容赦なく食いちぎり　鼻ひとつ残さずたちまち食べつくす
いまは首のなくなった兎の小さなからだに　てりかける月光
狼のからだも殆ど金色に光っているが　彼は月を見上げようともしない
急いで唸りながら兎のやわらかな胸を食べ出す
点々と地上に血をこぼしながら
さらに胸を　細い毛におおわれた尻を
（あおざめて拍手している私たち）
兎はもう四つの脚だけになった　曽て波よりも素早く
歌よりも軽く野を走った兎の脚　いまはかすかにヒクヒク動く
四つのやせた冷い棒だ
ようやく狼はゆっくり顔を上げる　そして石でも見るように私たちを見る
（ねえ　ほれぼれする姿だ　ふるえながらささやき合う私たち）

Wolves

We circle, watching the wolf
with a mouth full of blood, ravenous,
devouring a rabbit, ripping through
the pathetic creature's face

till even its nose is gone. Moonlight
shines on the headless corpse
and the burnished wolf
doesn't so much as look up

as it groans and gnaws
through the rabbit's soft breast—
drops of blood spattering the ground—
and further, into a thin-furred hip, while we—

our faces drained of colour—applaud,
the rabbit reduced to its legs: legs
that once ran swift as the tide; legs
that once leapt light as song; legs

狼は私たちを見つめ続ける　なにげなく　次第に凄まじく
私たちは不安になる　でもまた何故
（私たちは見物に来ただけだ　ちょっと見物に来ただけ）

狼の好きな少年がいた
いたずら好きでいつも私たちを笑わせる少年
彼は最前列でうっとりと狼を見ていた
狼はその彼にとびかかった　がっと押し倒し咽喉元に食いつく
ぼく　お前のファンなんだ……
弱々しくささやいて少年は絶命する
十一の若さ　まだ育ちきらぬからだのまま
なぜ彼を死なせてしまった　一体なぜ
（月光をあびて狼と向いあう私たち）

死んだ少年は私たちのものでなければならない

now shivered into four cold bones.
Slowly, the wolf lifts its head and regards us
like so many stones. We
whisper to each other, trembling in awe.

Gradually the wolf's deadpan gaze
gets a sense of us, fierce, intent. We
are fearful, without quite knowing why: we
only came to watch, just for a while...

but a boy—the wolf's biggest fan
and out to make us
laugh—is there at the front, where the wolf
leaps on him, savagely pinning him

to the ground. It has him by the throat
and won't let go, even as the boy—
with his last gasp—whispers
'You're my hero'. Eleven years old,

not even fully grown. Now it's us
in the spotlight, left
to face the wolf, the beloved
boy's death on our bewildered hands.

ISHIKAWA ITSUKO   55

ISHIKAWA ITSUKO
石川逸子

translated by

CAROL HAYES
キャロル・ヘイズ
&
RINA KIKUCHI
菊地利奈

娘の部屋

千鳥ケ淵にくる前の日
娘よ
あなたは発っていきました

からんとなった　あなたの部屋
洋服箪笥には　置いていった　古びた服
青いカーテンが揺れて
あなたは　いない

あなたは単に　この家から離れていっただけなのに
同じトウキョウの空の下で
元気に今日も窓を開けているだろうに
あなたの旅立ちの　辛さ

トカトカ階段を降りてくる足音のもう無いことが
なにげない笑い声の響かないことが

My Daughter's Room

The day before I visited the Chidorigafuchi
My daughter
You went and left home

Your room   completely empty
Your old clothes   left behind   in that chest of drawers
The blue curtains sway
You   are not here

You simply   removed yourself from this house
Under the same Tokyo sky
You'll be opening your window today too, as full of energy as always
Your departure   fills me with such pain

Your footsteps no longer clatter down the stairs
Your easy laughter no longer echoes around
Such emptiness
Fills my eyes with tears

Without you
In your room   I stand lost
That makes me wonder

こんなに虚ろで
涙の滲むことだったとは

あなたのいない
あなたの部屋に　ぼんやり佇ち
そして想った
赤紙がやってきた日の
母の気持

骨になってしまうかもしれない
わが子を　万歳で送る
母の気持

How those mothers must have felt
The day that red draft slip arrived

How those mothers must have felt
Sending their sons off   with a banzai
Sons, who will end as bones

石の碑

大きな石の碑が建っていました

「過まてる国の政策のため
無惨な骨となりし人たち　ここに眠る
ああ永久(とわ)に戦争許すまじ」
と刻まれているだろうか

昭和天皇の歌でした
「くにのためいのちささげしひとびとの
　　ことをおもへばむねせまりくる」

ほかでもない　あなたに
捧げられた　夥(おびただ)しい　いのち
「大君の醜(しこ)の御楯と身をなさば雲染む屍何か惜まん」
牛久保博一　東京医科大学出身
「戦友(とも)は征く我も又征く大君の御楯とならん生きて還らじ」
小野正明　享年十九歳

Stone Monument

There stood the large stone monument

Is this what is engraved here?

Due to unjust national policy

They became pitiful bones   they lie here

We must never again allow our nation to go to war

It was just a poem by His Majesty Emperor Showa

Whenever we ponder on those who dedicated their lives for the cause
of our nation,

Our heart aches with deep emotion

These   numberless   lives

Sacrificed for none other   than you

I become a shield for Your Majesty My Emperor

Although my blood splatters the clouds I have no regrets

By Ushikubo Hiroichi   Tokyo Medical University

My friends depart for war

I too depart

Your Majesty My Emperor we will be your shields

We will not come back alive

By Ono Masaaki   Deceased aged nineteen

「大君のみことしあれば天地（あめつち）のきはみの果も行き行き果てむ」

大森重憲　トラック諸島方面にて死す

あなたは知っているか
死の前夜　若者たちの胸に溢れた涙を
二度と生きられない命を思った
なお断腸の思いで母を偲んだ
あなたに捧げつつ

「告げもせで帰る戎衣（じゅうい）のわが肩にもろ手をかけて笑ます母かも」
知覧から飛び立っていった鷲尾克己よ
「送りくれし数々の文見つめつつ別れし去年（こぞ）の母が眼を恋ふ」
敗戦五日前に回天に搭乗していった水井淑夫よ

二度と還らない人たちのために
せめて　　一片のうたではなく
僧となって彼らの後世を弔いつつ
隠れ住んでほしかった　あなたには

64　　石川逸子

At your word Your Majesty My Emperor
I will go, go to the very edge of world, even to my death
By Oomori Shigenori   Died somewhere near the Truk Islands

Sacrificing themselves to you Your Majesty
Missing their mothers with heart wrenching sorrow
I think about those lives that can never live again
Your Majesty, have you thought about
The tears that overflowed the hearts of these young men
    each night before each death

    Smiling for me my mother places her hand on my uniformed shoulder
    I return to base saying nothing
You, who flew out from Chiran, Washio Katsumi

    Looking at the many many letters sent to me by my mother
    I thinking lovingly of her eyes when we parted last year
You, Mizui Toshio, who became a human torpedo five days before
    the surrender

For those men who can never again return home
At the very least   instead of writing that fragment of poetry
You, Your Majesty, should have become a monk and prayed for the
    peace of their souls
You should have lived in isolation   I wish you had

少女 2

一九四五年八月一五日
あなたの祖国が解放された日
あなたは病んで
もう起きあがれない身でした

散々にあなたを弄んできた
日本の軍人たちは
そそくさと軍用トラックで逃亡し
そのことさえ知らず
六人の姉さん達と
底冷えする小屋に横たわっていた　あなたでした
僅か一七歳のあなた
「勤労挺身隊」の裏の意味も知らずに
古里を離れたあなた
汽車に乗ってからは見張られ

Girl 2

15th August 1945
The day your motherland was liberated
You were so sick
No longer able to sit up

After abusing you so relentlessly
The Japanese soldiers
Ran off in their army trucks in mad haste
Yet you knew nothing of all this
Left with your six 'elder sisters'
Lying there in that tiny freezing hut   You
You, only seventeen years old
With no understanding of the hidden meaning of 'Voluntary Labour
    Corps'
You, left your home town

Under guard on the train
Later jolted roughly in the last truck of the convoy
Taken to that cold place   teeth chilled to the very root
Your untouched body still to ripen
Falls prey to a sabred officer

やがて軍用トラックの最後尾で揺すられて
歯の根も合わない　寒い地へ運ばれ
まだ蕾の清らかなからだは
サーベルつけた将校の餌食にされました

一日に　二十人　三十人
生きているのか　死んでいるのか
震えるほど寒いから　まだ生きているのでしょう
生理の日でも次々に軍人があらわれるとは
もうこの世ではないのでしょうか
拒めばなぐられ
ヒリヒリ腫れた頬が痛いから　やっぱり生きているのでしょう

ある日　からだのあちこちに
斑点ができ
下半身はただれ　辛く
性病になってしまった　あなた
〈ひどくなるとトラックに乗せられ

Each day   twenty   thirty men
Am I alive?   Am I dead?
Shaking with cold   so I must be still living
Even when I'm menstruating, soldiers arrive one after another
Am I no longer in the human world?
Beaten for any refusal
Swollen cheeks burning with pain   so I must be still living

One day   spots appeared
All over your body
Your lower body so inflamed   so painful
You   infected with venereal disease
'When it gets really bad we're sent off in a truck
 and dumped out on the empty plains'
You   terrified   by such whispered talk

Even then the soldiers continue to arrive
Your infection   worse day by day
Your body burningly feverish
 'Will it be me?   Will I fall prey to wolves?'
But on that one day   the Japanese army discarded you
Let's run away   quickly
The others call to you
I can't move, I'll stay here   with my sisters

曠野に放られてしまうそうだよ〉
ささやかれる噂に　脅えた　あなた

軍人たちはそれでもやってくる
あなたの病は　日に日に重くなり
からだはひどく熱っぽく
〈私　狼のエサになるんだろうか〉
そんな日に　日本軍はあなたを捨てました
逃げましょう　早く
誘う仲間に
動けないからここにいます　姉さんたちと一緒に
안녕히 가십시요（さようなら）
アンニョンヒ　カシプシ　ヨ
朝露のような涙をひとしずく　こぼした　あなた

それからのことは　わかりません
生きられたか
死んでしまったか
生きているなら　どこに

Annyeonghi kashipshiyo Farewell

You   let fall   a single tear like a morning dewdrop

What happened after that   nobody knows

Did you survive?

Did you die?

If alive   where are you?

If dead   where are you?

Seventeen years old

　　　'I thought I'd be nursing wounded soldiers.'

That's what they say you said one day   with such a face of
　　girlish innocence

So like a pink peach blossom

15th August 1945

'Having been able to safeguard and maintain the structure of the
　　Imperial State, We are always with ye, Our good and loyal subjects,
　　relying upon your sincerity and integrity.….'

Hearing His Majesty Emperor Showa's radio announcement

No more blackout regulations   No more air raids

Contradicting the beliefs of a patriotic daughter of the emperor

That twelve-year old me   was so relieved

But in that abandoned 'comfort women' station in Jilin

The six of you lying there unable to move   and you so emaciated

What happened to you?

Only the wind   bears witness.

死んでしまったなら　どこに

　一七歳
　〈怪我した兵隊さんのお世話をすると思ったの〉
ある日　ポツリといった顔は幼げで
桃の花のようだった　というけれど

一九四五年八月一五日
「朕ハ茲ニ国体ヲ護持シ得テ忠良ナル爾臣民ノ赤誠ニ信倚シ常ニ爾臣民ト共ニ在リ……」
昭和天皇の放送に
もう灯火管制はなくなった　空襲もないのだ　と
それまでの皇国少女が嘘のように
一二歳の私は　ほっとしていたけれど
がらんとした　吉林省とある兵営内の「慰安所」で
寝たきりの六人のあなたがたは　痩せこけたあなたは
どうなったか
知っているのは　風だけなのでしょうか

ITO HIROMI
伊藤比呂美

translated by

JEFFREY ANGLES
ジェフリー・アングルス

父の子宮あるいは一枚の地図

その部屋はいろんな瓶の中に
いろんな人体の部分がおしこめられていて
いろんな奇形も奇病もわたしたちは見ることができた
ほんとうはいろんな死体もそこで見ることができたが
男たちはそっちに行きたがらなかった
だから部分的な人体だけ見ることにした
人体の部分たちは液体の中で変色していって
もうきっと
けっしてよみがえらない

ほらこれがぼくの父の腕だと
乾きあがった腕をゆびさして男たちが言う
これが父の皮膚
男たちは皮膚病の皮膚をゆびさす
これが父の胃
潰瘍のある胃を男たちはゆびさす

Father's Uterus, or the Map

In that room various body parts
Are stuffed into various bottles
We saw various deformities, various strange diseases
We could have seen various dead bodies but
The men didn't want to go there
That's why all I saw were parts of bodies
Body parts that had changed color in the liquid
No chance
Of them coming back to life

Look, that's my father's arm
The men said pointing to an arm all dried up
That's my father's skin
The men pointed to a patch of skin ridden with disease
That's my father's stomach
The men pointed to a stomach with ulcers
Those are my father's testicles
The men pointed to testicles with elephantiasis
Those are my father's bones and spinal column
Those are my father's joints
Those are us, the children our father gave birth to

これが父の睾丸
象皮病の睾丸を男たちはゆびさす
これが父の骨と脊椎
これが父の指の関節
これが父の産んでくれたぼくたち
と水頭症の胎児たちをゆびさす
そしてこれがあなた
と癌の乳房をゆびさす
そしてこれが父の子宮だと
歯の生えた子宮をゆびさして男たちが言う
肉をかきわけて歯がいれつにならぶ
これは病気あるいは奇形だとわたしは
言いたいが言わない
これが父の子宮だ
ぼくたちは子どものころよく父に打擲された
これがぼくたちを折檻した残酷な子宮の歯だ
一人は号泣し
もう一人は踊りながら男たちが

The men pointed to fetuses with hydrocephalus

And that is you

The men pointed to a breast with cancer

And that is my father's uterus

The men pointed to a uterus that had grown teeth

There were a row of teeth pushing the flesh aside

I wanted to say

This is a disease, a deformity

But I did not

That is my father's uterus

When we were boys, our father often thrashed us

Those are the cruel uterine teeth that punished us

One began to sob

Another began to dance

Meanwhile the men suddenly broke the bottle

With the uterus with the teeth

Regardless of whether it was their father's or anyone else's

Regardless of whether it was the result of disease or deformity

The bottle broke

Tears and medicinal fluid

Teeth and glass shards

I thought

These actions are merely maudlin

歯の生えた子宮の瓶をいきなりぶち割る

父のでも誰のでも病気でも奇形でも

とにかく瓶は割れて

涙と薬液が、歯とガラス片が

こんな行為は感傷にすぎないとわたしは

思っているが言わない

「地図をひろげてどこかへ行きたいと思うが、

地図中いたるところに父がたちあがる。

わたしは父のいない場所をさがすのにやっきになる。

父はたちあがる。

父は地図上のどこにでも、わたしがゆびさせばそこに父はたちあがる」

というどこかの父娘の話をして聞かせながら男はわたしに一枚の地図をくれた

外国語で表記してある地図だ

地図に描かれた土地の形は知っている

土地の名前も知ってるが

その言語は読めない

男には読める

だから地図を見るたびにわたしはその言語に

But I did not say anything

'When I open the map and think about where I want to go

There is my father, standing everywhere on the map

I become desperate to find someplace he's not

My father stands everywhere

My father stands everywhere on the map, I point and he's there'

I am telling this story I heard somewhere of father and daughter

When one of the men gives me a map

A map marked in a foreign tongue

I know the contours of the land

I know the names of places too but

I can't read the language

The men can read it however

So whenever I look at the map

That language

The men who read that language

Watch me with tactful eyes

Of course the man who gave me the map

And immediately started to stand watch

Regretted his actions

He writhed with regret

Be quiet (I wished)

言語を読める男に

巧妙に監視される

もちろん地図をくれた男はたちまち監視する自分を
後悔して
懺悔のあまりのたうちまわっている
静かになれ（とわたしはねがう）
死んでしまえ（とわたしはねがう）
考えられるかぎりのいちばんつまらない死に方で男は死にたい
かんだガムを床になすりつけるとか
爆風でとつぜん消えるとか
餓死するとか
それなのに男はわたしを監視するために地図をくれる
いつでもどこでも地図の中に立ちあがる
瓶の中からでもよみがえってみせる
でも男は後悔している
後悔のあまりのたうちまわっている
そっとしておくしかない

Drop dead (I wished)

He should die the dullest death imaginable

Dashing chewed gum to the floor or

Disappearing suddenly in a burst of wind or

Starving to death or something

Still the man gives me a map in order to keep watch

No matter when, no matter where, he is standing there in the map

He appears even inside the bottles, come back to life

But the man regrets

He writhes with regret

No choice but to leave him be

Call out and

Immediately he is standing there

He is going to thrash me

The man's blood vessels brim to overflowing

The same way they have dozens, hundreds of times

Father, older brother

Husband, lover, teacher, whatever I call him

声をかけると
たちまちたちあがり
わたしを打擲するからだ
何十回も何百回もくりかえされたやり方で
男の血管がそこにみなぎる
父あるいは兄
夫、恋人、先生、なんとでも彼を呼べる

YAKISOBA

ある日私は呼び止められた
マーケットで、日系人のあつまる
居酒屋がある、モールの片隅に
そこには切り干し大根やひじき煮なんかがあり
その隣はカレー屋で
そこにはカツカレーなんかがあり
その隣は日本式のケーキ屋で
そこにはイチゴのショートケーキがある
秋になるとモンブランが出る
その隣がマーケット
なかでは年取った女が働いている
宣伝販売である
彼女は叫んでいる、なまり切った英語で
年頃は六〇代後半、日本で生まれて日本で育った
若いときにここに来た、この生活の方が長い
もう帰らない

伊藤比呂美

Yakisoba

One day

At a supermarket where all the Japanese-Americans go

Someone called out and stopped me in my tracks

At the corner of the mall is an izakaya

Where they serve simmering kiriboshi daikon and hijiki

Next to that is a curry shop

Where they serve katsu curry and other things

Next to that is a Japanese-style cake shop

Where they serve strawberry shortcake

And in the fall, Mont Blanc

Next to that is the Japanese supermarket

An old woman works there in promotion

She yells in English with a strong accent

Probably in her late sixties, probably born and raised in Japan

Came here when she was young, probably lived here longer

Never to return

She uses only Japanese with her family

When she speaks in Japanese

Her children and grandchildren respond only in English

彼女は使うひたすら日本語を家族にたいして

彼女が話しかけると日本語で

子どもも孫も返してくるひたすら英語で

今日、まさに今、彼女は叫び、次のように

呼び止めた、一人の女を

ちょっとおくさん寄ってってぐっつそーすがいんくるーでっどよ！ *

それは私である、呼び止められた（彼女が呼び止めた）

私は考えた、立ち止まりながら

いったいぜんたいだれをこの地球上で

あの呼びかけは呼び止めようとしているのか、どんな人間を？

どんな背景を？　どんな性の？　どんな生活のただ中にいる？

なにを共有したがっているのか、呼びかけた相手と？

そしてそれはまさに私である

私こそ共有している

その言語の、性の、年齢の、立場の、興味の、金銭感覚の

彼女の狙いさだめている、などと考えながら

手に取り、彼女の差し出すやきそばの一盛りを

懐かしく味わい、それを

Today, just now, she yelled

And stopped a woman

'*Chotto okusan yottette!* Good sauce *ga* included *yo!*'

I was the one she stopped

My mind spun as I stopped

What the heck, who on earth

Is her yelling meant to stop?

What kind of person, what background, what gender, what station
    in life?

What does she want to say to the person she stops?

Aren't I the one?

The one who shares those things? Was I the one who shared

The language, gender, age, station in life, interests, financial values

This lady was targeting? That was what was going through my mind

As I took a sample of her yakisoba

And tasted it with so much nostalgia

I took a bag of yakisoba, thinking, '*Ara, kore wa* rather cheap *da wa ne!*'

Scrutinized it

And threw it into the shopping cart

All of the what

That are there?

アラこれはらざぁちーぷだわねなどと思いながら手に取り、それを
ためつすがめつし
投げ入れたのである、それを、カートの中に
有る程の*
何を？
どこに？
ありがと、と彼女が
いいええ、と私が
女がいる、ここに
生き替り死に替り
つながる、つぎの女に
何十人となく何百人となく何千人となく
何世代となく何十世代となく

* Good sauce ga included yo!
* Korewa rather cheap dawane.
* 漱石

Arigatō, she says

Iie, I say

Here is a woman

Who comes back alive, who comes back dead

Who connects with the next woman

With tens and hundreds and thousands of women

With generations, dozens of generations down the line

鰻と鯰

へんなメールがきたのである
Hello to you ごあいさつ申し上げます
My name is S-da 私の名前はS田
and I'm a poet そしてわたしは詩人
writing from western M M州西部から書いています
I am wondering 思うのですが
if you might have any もしやあなたが何かおもちではないか
recommendations or suggestions 推薦ないしは提案を
of places to visit in and around Kumamoto 熊本の周辺で訪れるべきところ
わたしは返信した。 何をあなたはわたしにしてほしいですか
これはわたしの第一回目、メールをもらい、話しかけられたのは
熊本にいるという理由だけで、わたしのことを知らない人から
たぶんS田は、わたしがナイスにも
じゃーうちにお泊まりなさいということを期待していたのだと思う
そうは問屋がおろしません
熊本の夏は堪えがたく暑く

Eels and Catfish

A strange e-mail arrived

Hello to you

My name is Shimoda

And I'm a poet

Writing from Western Maine

I am wondering

If you might have any

Recommendations or suggestions

Of places to visit in or around Kumamoto

I responded. What do you want of me?

That was the first time I had received an email, someone had
    approached me

Someone I didn't know, just because I live in Kumamoto

I imagined this Shimoda fellow was hoping I'd be nice

And say, well, why don't you stay with me?

But that is too presumptuous

Kumamoto summers are unbearably hot

Japanese houses are even hotter and more humid than the
    horrible weather outside

I hated the thought of taking in a complete stranger

日本の家屋は酷熱の屋外よりもさらに蒸し暑く
見知らぬ人を家のなかに入れるのは絶対にいやだ
しかしわたしもまた過去の日々に
このように見知らぬ土地にたどりつき
土地の人々のめしを食い
土地の人々の時間をつかった
恩は返さねばならぬと思いすまし
くそ暑い、くそ忙しい中を町中に出ていって
拾い上げたのである
そしたら一人ではなく二人であった
若い男と若い女であった
そこで二人を更科そばに案内し
これがいちばんオーセンティックな
ジャパニーズフード、この町で
などと嘘っぱちもとい真摯な意見を語り、メニューを読み上げ
わからないからまかせるといわれ
好き嫌いもきかずに穴子天もりにきめて
（東京風でたいへんうまい店だがここはあいにく熊本で

94　伊藤比呂美

But there was a day that I too had arrived like that

In an unfamiliar land

I ate the food people there gave me

I squandered the time people there provided

I felt like I had to repay my debt

So although terribly busy, I went into town in the horrific heat

And picked him up

But he was not one person but two

A young man and a young woman

I took them both out to eat some soba

As I read the menu out loud, I convinced them

This is the most *oosentikku*

Japaniizu fuudo in this town

Although that is not entirely true

We don't know, we'll just leave it up to you, they said

Not bothering to ask their likes and dislikes, I settled on sea eel
tempura with soba

(The restaurant was in the Tokyo style and was really good

But we were in Kumamoto, and unfortunately it didn't have mustard-
stuffed lotus roots

Or boiled green onions with sour miso, or raw horsemeat

The kinds of local delicacies one would expect in Kumamoto)

その店には
熊本ならばあってしかるべきからし蓮根も
人文字のぐるぐるも馬刺しもなかったのだ)
そばがくるのをまつうちに二人は話しはじめた
われわれは探している、場所を、N瀬と呼ぶ
そこは、私のおじいさんの住んでいた土地
われわれは調べた、そこを、そしてみつけ出した
あれを、その地名は消滅してしまったということを
われわれは思っている、行くのである、取って、バスを
今日これから、と
とりあえず自分たちで解決しようというその態度に
わたしはたいへん好感を持った
その上かれらはたいへん若かった
そして考えてみればただの詩人ではなかった
日系人
まあお待ちなさいとわたしはおしとどめ
B場さんに電話をしたのである
B場さんは友人である

The two began to talk as we waited

We are looking for a place, a place called Nakanose

That was where my grandfather lived

We looked it up and found it

That place name is gone but

We think we'll go there anyway, take a bus

Today after we get done, they said

Their attitude, their wish to solve problems on their own

Gave me a good impression

Plus, they were both really young

And come to think of it, he was not just a poet

He was a Japanese-American

Hold on a minute, I said

I called Baba-san

Baba-san is a friend of mine

A long time ago when I lost everything

When I was left behind, defenseless in Kumamoto

He came up to me with a smile

And we have been doing things together ever since

As a civil servant, he has been transferred all over the prefecture

So he should know just about all the place names in Kumamoto

昔わたしがすべてをなくし
熊本にとり残されてとほうにくれておったとき
ニコニコしながら近づいてきてくれた
それ以来ともに活動してきた友人なのである
公務員として県内をさんざん転任し
熊本の地名ならどこでも知っている
そして幸運であった、まっ昼間、Ｂ場さんにつながった
Ｈバイパスを行って
Ｋ川を渡ったあたりじゃないかと思うのですが
ちょっと待ってくださいと、調べますからといわれて
彼らは穴子天もり
わたしは蓴菜そばを食べておると
Ｂ場さんから電話が来た
たしかにＨバイパスを行ってＫ川を渡ったあたり
たしかに現在その地名は消失し
「うなぎのとくながＮ瀬本店」にかろうじてその名が残っている
そこの電話番号をナビに入れて行けばかならず行き着く
そしてなんと

And as luck would have it, I got through to him in the middle of
  the day

I think you go along the Hamasen Bypass

And cross the Kase River, but hold on

I'll look it up, he told me

As they were eating their sea eel tempura and soba

And I was eating my junsai soba

Baba-san called back

I was right, go along the Hamasen Bypass, cross the Kase River,
  and it's there

He was right, the place name no longer exists

The name has been all but forgotten, it remains only in the name of
  a single restaurant

  Tokunaga Eels, Nakanose Main Branch

Put the telephone number in your GPS and you'll be sure to get there

Then Baba-san specified

That place is in Catfish

And so we went

Leaving town, even after leaving town

There were rows upon rows of dull city streets

Then suddenly our path went down a narrow lane with nothing on it

Then the narrow lane gave way to a broad street

そこが鯰でありますとB場さんに的確な指示をされ
そのとおり走り出したわれわれである
町を抜けるまでは、　抜けてからも
つまらない町並みがつづいた
道はとつぜん何もない細道に入りこみ
細道から出ると広々とした道になった
Hバイパスと呼ばれる道であった
つまらない町並みであった
コンビニやファミレスがつづくのであった
どこにでもあるチェーン店がつづくのであった
けばけばしい看板がつづくのであった
パチンコ店がわめき立てるのであった
大きなモールがとつぜん出現するのであった
駐車場は果てしなく広がっているのであった
K川にかかる橋をわたった
橋のたもとに鰻やがあった
あたりには鰻のにおいがたちこめていた
裏はいちめんの田んぼであった

100　伊藤比呂美

That was the Hamasen Bypass

Lined with boring city buildings

Rows of convenience stores and family restaurants

Rows of chain stores just like you might find anywhere

Rows of gaudy signs

Pachinko parlors raising a racket

Suddenly a large mall appeared

The parking lot stretching on endlessly

We crossed the bridge across the Kase River

At the foot of the bridge was a restaurant that specialized in eel

The aroma of barbequed eel filled the air

Beyond the restaurant was nothing but rice paddies

I stopped the car at the embankment and he walked around

Smoke was coming out of the eel restaurant

The air was full of a delicious scent

Neither he nor his wife knew

That scent came from the barbequed eels

That the scent alone makes you want to eat and eat

When his grandfather was nine

He set out alone for America

His family had already gone, the reason

土手に車をとめると、彼はあたりを歩き回った

鰻やの建物は煙っていた

実にうまそうなにおいがむんむんした

このにおいだけで白いめしがいくらでも食べられることを彼は

においだけで白いめしがいくらでも食べられることを彼は

知らないのである、彼の妻も知らないのである

彼のおじいさんは九歳のとき

一人でアメリカに渡った

家族は先に渡っていった、あとに

一人で残ったのは病気であったからだ

病気は癒えて、九歳の少年が

一人で熊本から大分へ出て船に乗って横浜へ向かい

横浜で乗り換えて桑港にたどり着いた

一人で

むこうの田んぼのなかに墓地が見えた

われわれは可能でありますか行くことがあそこに？

と彼がおずおずと言い出した

可能です、しましょう車をとって、行けますあそこへ

He was left behind alone was because he was sick

After he recovered, the nine year-old boy

Went alone from Kumamoto to Oita, then set sail for Yokohama

Changed boats in Yokohama, then arrived in San Francisco

All alone

In the rice paddies across the way was a cemetery

Can we go in there?

He asked hesitantly

Sure, let's do it

I told him we could take the car and go over there

The narrow farming road went on and on

The water flowed alongside unbroken

There was a board forming a bridge from the road to the cemetery

There were more than ten gravestones

And there I found it, a gravestone marked Shimoda, the same name

It must be a relative, a direct one or not, I could not be sure

But looking at the wide-open landscape around the rice paddies

I could imagine how stubborn society must be

I could imagine his had not been the main branch but an offshoot
    of the family

A branch family goes out into the world, it splits off

とわたしが請け合った
細い農道がつづいていた
縦横無尽に水が流れて
板が架けられ道からその墓地に渡れるようになっていた
墓石が十数基
そのなかにみつけたのである、S田という彼と同じ名字の墓を
縁はあるだろうが直系かどうか、しかしこの
田んぼのひろがる風景を見ておれば
地域社会の頑なさも、本家とか分家とかそういう区別も
なんとなく想像でき
枝分かれした分家の一家が外に出ていき、離散していき
さらにその末裔の男は
ここに一人の九歳の少年となり
太平洋を渡り横浜から大分にそして熊本にたどり着き
たった一人で
対峙している
S田家累代之墓に
脇に建っているのは

And the descendant of that family

Like a nine year-old boy

Crosses the Pacific, goes from Yokohama to Oita, then arrives in
  Kumamoto

All alone

And stands face to face

With the grave where generations of the Shimoda family are buried

Next to that

Is the grave of Shimoda Takayuki

An army sergeant who died in the 1940s

Killed on the battlefield in his early twenties

(I took a photo of it on my cell phone, just now as I searched for it

A picture of my dead aunt's face suddenly came up on the screen

My aunt who died just recently, I did not go to the funeral

My cousin sent it, I wanted to erase it, but I could not bring myself
  to do it

I keep my aunt, her dead face, her corpse in my cell phone)

On the far side of the road was Catfish

The name of the place was written clear as day on the telephone pole

  Catfish, Kashima Town, Mashiki County

In ancient times, a caldera formed in Aso and collected lots of water

A big, big lake formed there, and a big, big catfish lived inside

S田K孝之墓

陸軍伍長昭和何年どこそこ、二〇代初めの戦死であった

（わたしはそれを携帯で写真にとったので画像を検索していると

今、画面にいきなり伯母の死に顔があらわれた

こないだ死んだ伯母だ、わたしは葬式に行かなかった

従弟が送ってきたそれを消去しきれずにいる

携帯のなかに伯母を、死に顔を、死体を持ちつづけている）

道の向こうは鯰である

電信柱にははっきりとM郡K町鯰と書いてある

大昔、阿蘇にカルデラができて水がたまった

大きな、大きな湖になった、大きな、大きな

土着の鯰が生きていた、タケイワタツノミコトがやってきて支配した

タケイワタツノミコトはその足で湖を蹴やぶった

水はあふれ出て流れ流れ、流れ流れ

流れ流れた

のみこんだ

死に絶えた

土着の鯰が生きていた

The god Takeiwatatsu-no-mikoto came and ruled over the area

He kicked the side of the lake with his feet

The water overflowed and ran out, running, running, running all
over the place

It ran and ran

It swallowed everything up

Everything perished

The native catfish was alive though

Takeiwatatsu-no-mikoto killed it by cutting it up

He chopped it up

Into little pieces

The place was covered in blood, but the water washed it away

A piece of the catfish was washed to this distant place

So this place is called Catfish

They call it that even now

A tiny, mud-coloured frog jumped

From the top of the plank bridge down below

Tiny, mud-coloured frogs jumped in the muddy water

The water had retreated but the trees and grasses

And vines had grown, covering traces of blood

Covering the slaughter

タケイワタツノミコトはそれも斬り殺した
ずたずたに
斬り殺した
血だらけになった、水に洗い流された
遠くのこの地に鯰の一片が流れついた
ここが鯰
いまでもそう呼ぶ
渡り板の上から下へ
泥色の小蛙がしきりに跳ねた
泥水のなかで泥色の小蛙たちが跳ねた
水がひいて、木々が、草々が
蔓を伸ばして血の跡を
殺戮をおおい隠した
みどりの田んぼを青鷺がゆうゆうと歩いている
車を発進させたとき
日系人が振り向いて
自分の根にむかって手を振った

A blue heron walked slowly in the green rice paddy

When I started the car

The Japanese-American turned

Looked over his shoulder

And waved in the direction of his own past

HIRATA TOSHIKO
平田俊子

translated by

CAROL HAYES
キャロル・ヘイズ
&
RINA KIKUCHI
菊地利奈

一月七日

旅に出よう
詩を書くためにだけ旅に出よう
そう決めたのに 一回目から早くも挫折
夕暮れどきの丸ノ内線に
臆面もなく腰掛けている
中吊りの　女性雑誌の広告は
横書きのピンクの文字が目立つ
わたしとの接点何もなく
じっと見ていると
自分が男になった気分

男になろう
旅に出るのが難しいなら
詩を書くためにだけ男になろう
そう決めたわたしの耳に
「寂しいから犬のトルソーを買ったの」という細い声

The Seventh of the First Month

I'll go on a journey

I'll go on a journey just to write poetry

I'd made my decision, but I failed from the very first step

It's early evening on the Marunouchi line

I sit without a shred of guilt

Hanging adverts   from woman's magazines

The pink horizontal letters catch my eye

They mean nothing to me

Staring at them

I feel I've become a man

I'll become a man then

If it's so hard to leave on a journey

I'll become a man just so I can write poetry

Just as I decided, I heard a delicate voice

'I was so lonely I bought a dog's torso'

So that's it   when they're lonely women buy torsos

then they embrace the torso they've bought when they sleep

そうか　寂しいとき女はトルソーを買うのか
買ったトルソーを抱いて寝るのか
トルソー＝首及び四肢を欠く胴体だけの塑像　（広辞苑）
そんなものを買うのが喜びなのか
男のからだも女のからだも
けれどもゆれを感じる場所は
ひとりずつ
微妙に違っている

男の駅
女の駅
男の駅
女の駅
電車は順に停車する
男の駅
女の駅
男の駅

a torso = the soft clay trunk of the body independent of the neck or
    limbs (Kōjien dictionary)

So buying a thing like that gives them pleasure!

Men's bodies women's bodies

The Marunouchi line carries all equally

But how each body feels the rocking

Is individual

Is subtly different

Man Station

Woman Station

Man Station

Woman Station

The train stops in turn

Man Station

Woman Station

Man Station

Woman Station

女の駅
車体は次第に赤みを帯びる
男の駅
女の駅
男の駅
女の駅
いつしかお客は犬のトルソー

The carriages gradually become tinged with red

Man Station

Woman Station

Man Station

Woman Station

All unnoticed, the passengers are dog's torsos

十三月七日

七十をいくつか過ぎた人のために
化粧品を買いに行く
シミとシワをきれいに隠してくれる
液体のファンデーションを

初めて会った頃
この人はまだ二十代だった
あまり幸せではない結婚をして
不機嫌な顔で
赤ん坊のおしめを替えていた

三十代のこの人も
楽しそうには見えなかった
カタカタカタとミシンを踏んでは
わけのわからないものを作っていた

The Seventh of the Thirteenth Month

I go to buy makeup

For a woman a few years over seventy

Liquid foundation

To hide her wrinkles and blemishes

When I first met her

She was only in her twenties

Rather unhappily married

Changing her baby's nappy

With a grumpy face

Even in her thirties

She didn't look happy

Clank, clack, clank, her foot to the sewing pedal

Endlessly producing weird things

In her forties, this woman

Secretly read her daughter's diary

Opened letters addressed to her daughter without asking

四十代のこの人は
娘の日記をこっそり読んで
娘にきた手紙を勝手に開けた
娘が幸せにならないよう呪いをかけた
呪いは実によく効いたので
娘は毎日頭痛で悩んだ

五十代のこの人を知らない
わたしは遠く家を出たから

六十代のこの人も知らない
一度も帰らなかったから

二十数年ぶりに会ったこの人は
七十をいくつか過ぎていて
母というより老人だった
自分の母が

Placed a curse on her daughter to stop her ever being happy

The curse was so effective

Her daughter suffered terrible headaches day after day

I know nothing of her fifties

Because I moved far from home

I know nothing of her sixties either

Because I never once went home

Meeting up with her after more than twenty years

She was a few years over seventy

Less a mother and more an old woman

I was a bit shocked

Because I'd never thought about the day

When my own mother would become an old woman

Now in my forties, I

Read the shopping lists she's written

Open the bills addressed to her without asking

Then make the payments

老人になる日がくるとは思わなかったので
ちょっと驚いた

四十代になったわたしは
この人の書いた買い物メモを読み
この人宛ての請求書を勝手に開けて
支払いをすませる
七十を過ぎたこの人のために
化粧品を買いに行く
四十代の頃のこの人を
まだ許してはいないのに

シミやシワをきれいに隠す
液体のファンデーション
わたしはそれで
自分のこころを
隠そうとしているのかもしれない

I go to buy makeup

For this woman over seventy

Though I still haven't forgiven

Her for her forties

The liquid foundation

Beautifully hides her wrinkles and blemishes

Maybe I'm using it

To try and hide

My inner self

二十四月七日

「この先、ゆれますのでご注意ください」
のどかな声がバスのなかを泳ぐ
それは困ります、運転手さん
わたしは洗面器を抱えています
洗面器のなかには金魚が一匹
バスがゆれると水をひきつれて
金魚が飛び出してしまいます

「この先、ゆれますのでご注意下さい」
ゆらすのはあなた
それともバス自身ですか
風邪の予防には注射をします
ゆれを防ぐ注射はないのですか
実はわたくし乗り物に酔います
この先、吐きますのでご注意下さい

The Seventh of the Twenty-Fourth Month

'There will now be some bumpiness, please take care'

The calm voice swam through the bus

That will be a problem, driver

I'm holding a washing basin

In the basin is a goldfish

If the bus sways, drawing the water along

The goldfish will jump out

'There will now be some bumpiness, please take care'

It's you making it bumpy

Or is it the bus doing it?

We have an injection for flu prevention

Is there any injection to prevent bumpiness?

To tell the truth I suffer from motion sickness

'There will now be some vomiting, please take care'

I don't have anything like those sick bags

Though I do have a washing basin

But because it has a goldfish swimming in it, I can't use that

エチケット袋なんて持ってません
洗面器ならありますけど
金魚が泳いでいますから使うわけにはいきません
ゲロまみれの金魚なんて
あなた見たくないでしょう？

みちゆきって名前の知り合いが二人いました
ひとりは小学校の若い教師で
ひとりは高校の文芸部の先輩でした
親は何を考えてそんな名前をつけたのでしょうね
二人はその後道行きをしたかしら
たぶんしなかったと思いますよ
子どもはなかなか親の期待どおりには
いきませんもの

この金魚の名前もみちゆきっていうんですよ
ほら、口をぱくぱくさせて
何ていってるんでしょうね

A goldfish covered in spew

You don't want to see that, do you?

I knew two people called Michiyuki or 'Journey'

One was a young teacher at my primary school

The other was a senior in my writing club at high school

What on earth were their parents thinking giving
   them a name like that?

I wonder whether either of them actually went on a journey.

No, they probably didn't

Children don't tend to follow their parents expectations

Do they?

This goldfish is called Michiyuki too, you know.

Look, his mouth is popping open and shut

What's he saying, do you think?

To die?   Not to die?

Not to die?   To die?

That's what it sounds like to me

That's right, me, I've been asked to join a michiyuki
   love journey to death

死ぬか　死なぬか
死なぬか　死ぬか
わたしにはそう聞こえます
ええ、道行きを持ちかけられてるんです、わたし

「この先、ゆれますのでご注意下さい」
洗面器から金魚が飛び出し
バスの窓からわたしが飛び出す
それも道行きになるんでしょうか
全身打撲で
死ぬか　死なぬか
死なぬか　死ぬか
ずいぶん元気な道行きだあね

この先、ゆれませんのでご注意下さい
この先、死にますのでご注意ください
この先、死にませんのでご注意ください

'There will now be some bumpiness, please take care'

The goldfish leaps out of the washing basin

I leap out of the bus window

Can this be called a love journey to death too?

The cause of death is excessive bruising

To die?　　　　Not to die?

Not to die?　　　　To die?

What an energetic michiyuki!

'There will now be no bumpiness, please take care'

'There will now be some death, please take care'

'There will now be no death, please take care'

KAWAGUCHI HARUMI
川口晴美

translated by

MELINDA SMITH

メリンダ・スミス

&

RINA KIKUCHI

菊地利奈

半島の地図

夏に歩いた海沿いの道を
指でたどる一人の夜
秋の紙はひんやり滑らかに
乾いている
そこからはもうどこへも行けない半島の先端で
立ちどまり見あげた空の下
あふれこぼれていた水分は
いったいどこに仕舞われてしまったのだろう
波が削り取っていったという離れ島が
あのとき沖に光っていたけれど
地図には載っていない
（ミズシマ）
記されなかった名を発音する唇が微かに
震えながら開かれるから
指は紙を離れ
秋のテーブルの葡萄をひと粒つまむ

Map of the Peninsula

The path I walked in summer follows the sea

—at night, alone, I trace it with my finger

This autumn paper is pleasantly cool, smooth,

dried out

Just there, at the tip of the peninsula, where I couldn't go any further,

where I stopped still and looked up, beneath the sky

—that wetness which welled up, spilled over,

where on earth did it dry up to?

They say the waves have been at the lone offshore island, wearing
  it away;

that day, it was glinting there in the open sea

but on this map it is nowhere to be found

'Wet Island'

My lips, pronouncing the unrecorded name

quiver slightly as they open, and so

my finger leaves the paper

and plucks a single grape from the bunch on the autumn table

Sealed inside,

the sweet wet young juice has deepened

塞がれて
あまく苦く深まった水を
夏のくちづけに似せて唇へ運ぶと
夜の光を連れて滴り
半島のような腕をたどって
冷えた地図に
わたしの熱を小さくまるく記していった

I bring it to my lips, I make it feel like summer's mouth is on mine

it pulls the glimmer of night along with it and drips,

trickling along my arm—my peninsula—

and dropping onto the cooled map

records my fever with a small round mark.

席

夕暮れのレストランの二階で窓際のテーブルに座って
あまいお酒をひとくち飲むと
狭い通りをはさんだ向かいのビルの
おなじ高さにある喫茶店の窓際の席では誰かがコーヒーを飲んでいる
知らない横顔だけれど
わたしもまえにあの席でコーヒーを飲んだことがある
今日はたまたまこちら側にいるだけで
あちら側でコーヒーを飲んでいるのがわたしであってもおかしくはない
あれはわたしだったかもしれない

ずいぶんまえに遠い国で船に乗って川を下っていたとき
川辺に繁茂する植物のかげに男の子がひとり立っているのが見えた
ぼんやり船を見送る裸の上半身が濃く日に焼けているのがわかって
すぐに見えなくなった
あの子は一生べつの国に行くことはないかもしれない
もしかしたら生まれた村よりほかの場所を見ることもないかもしれない

My Seat

At dusk, I sit at a window table on the second floor of this
   restaurant

I take a sip of sweet wine

In the building facing this one, which juts out into the narrow
   street,

in the coffee shop at the same height, in the window seat,
   someone is drinking coffee

It is a profile I don't know

but I too have drunk coffee sitting in that seat

Today it is just by chance I am on this side

It would not be strange at all if I were the one drinking coffee
   over there

Perhaps that was actually me

Long ago, in a far country, I was on a boat coming down a river

In the shade of the thick wild growth on the bank I could see
   a boy standing alone

I made him out, absent-mindedly watching the boat move off,
   his naked upper body deeply tanned by the sun,

and straight away I could no longer see him

This boy may never go to another country his whole life

あの子とわたしはたった一度すれちがって
きっと二度と会わない
でも
わたしはあの子だったかもしれない
通り過ぎてゆく船に乗っている方がわたしだったのはたまたまで
川辺の村で一生を過ごす男の子に生まれていたとしてもおかしくはない
それはどんな感じがするだろう

わたしではないわたしよ
今日のコーヒーはおいしいか
川は穏やかに広々と流れているか
あまいお酒はこの体を流れ落ちてどこか見えないところへ染み込み
滲んでゆく
向かいの喫茶店の下の八百屋には明かりが灯り
ならんだ秋の果物のいくつもの形と色を輝かせはじめている

He may see no other place besides the village where he was born.

We passed each other just the once, this boy and I

We will almost certainly never meet again

but

perhaps I was him

It was just by chance I was the one who was on the boat passing
through

It would not be strange at all if I had been born a boy who passes
his whole life in a village on a riverbank

I wonder what that would feel like

Hey there, me who is not me,

is the coffee good today?

Is the river flowing wide and calm?

The sweet wine will flow down through this body and on
to somewhere we can't see, it will soak in

and spread out

On the floor below the coffee shop across the way, in the
greengrocer's, the lights are coming on.

The rows and rows of autumn fruit, their numberless colours
and shapes, begin to glow.

おかえり

誕生日おめでとう、と帰ってきた男がにっこり差し出したのはひとかかえもある箱で
反射的に受け取りながら予想外の重さに二、三歩よろめいてありがとうを
言うタイミングを逸してしまったけれどそれはわたしの誕生日が九ヶ月以上も先で
いっしょに暮らして何年にもなる男が間違うわけはないのだからもしかしたら
自分が記憶違いをしているのだろうかと一瞬考えたから
だけどもちろんそんなはずはない　にっこり
ばりばり包装紙を破り開くと水槽が
あらわれる　誕生する
でもからっぽ
ここにはきれいな熱帯魚もかわいい亀もすてきなカメレオンもいないから困って
とりあえず　映らなくなったテレビのかわりにテレビ台に置いてみると意外と似合う
おなじようなものかもしれない
そういえば　ずいぶん前に壊れたテレビを男と二人で抱えて粗大ゴミ置き場に
捨てたあのときはコドモを森に捨てるみたいで何度も振り向いてから二人で
走った夜明けの空の壊れものめいた青が肌にうつっていついつまでもとれない気がした
着替えた男はテレビ台の前のソファで缶ビールを開ける

Welcome Home

Happy Birthday! He came home with a box, more than an armful, and held it out to me, grinning.

Instinctively taking it from him and staggering a little at the unexpected weight

I messed up the timing of saying Thank you but this was because my birthday was over nine months away

—and since there is no question that this man who has been living with me for years would mistake the date,

I thought perhaps

just for a moment, that I myself was misremembering it

but that is, of course, unlikely   <grin>

I tear open the wrapping paper with gusto, and a glass aquarium

appears   is born

But it is empty

We don't own any beautiful tropical fish, cute turtles, gorgeous chameleons. I don't know what to do with it

To start with   I try putting it on top of the TV unit, where our television that stopped working used to be. It goes there unexpectedly well.

Perhaps they are the same kind of thing

In saying that   that time the two of us carried the long-ago broken TV in our arms to the large waste drop-off

to throw it away, we looked back at it again and again, as if we had

隣に座ってからっぽの水槽をいっしょに眺めるのもいいだろうけどせっかくだから

入ってみることにした

右足で跨ぎ左足をおさめ　微かにきしむ音がしたのは水槽かテレビ台かわたしか

膝を抱えるかたちでまるくなるとちょうどよくあてはまる

ウレシイコンナノ欲シカッタンダと言ったのはわたしかテレビ台か水槽か

ひんやり真新しい水に触れるようで硝子板がきゅうっと腕や足裏に吸いつく

意外と　いい

男は笑ってビールを飲みテレビを見ていたときとおなじ顔でぼんやり水槽を見ている

パジャマになってから何となくまた入ったらそのまま気持ちよく眠ってしまったので

当然のなりゆきとして次の日からそこがわたしの巣になり

外から戻るとただいまと言いながら鞄を投げ出し服を脱ぎ捨ておやすみなさいと水槽に

入る

きゅうつ

帰って来た男は静かにソファに座り開けた缶ビールを飲み干しながら眺める

眠っているわたし

からっぽの水槽

それとも映らなくなったもうないテレビの画面

ぼんやりして

abandoned a *child* in the woods,

and we ran, the two of us. The blue of the dawn sky lit up my skin
like a broken screen and I felt as if the colour would never come off

He has changed out of his work clothes, and opens a can of beer on
the sofa in front of the TV unit

It might be nice to sit next to him and stare together at the empty
aquarium, but since this is a special occasion

I decide to try getting inside it

Straddling with my right leg, guiding my left leg in   what was it
made that faint creaking sound? The aquarium? The TV unit? Me?

When I hug my knees and make myself round, I fill it out just right

I'm so happy. This is just what I wanted. Who said that? Me?
The TV unit? The aquarium?

The glass panels kiss the skin of my arms and the soles of my feet,
like cool fresh water

It is unexpectedly   good

He is smiling, drinking his beer, looking at the aquarium with the
same face he used to watch the TV with. Nothing in his head

I changed into my pyjamas, and climbed in again without really
thinking. I was so comfortable like that I fell fast asleep. And so

as if it were the natural course of things, from the next day on
    it became my nest

Every time I come back after going out I say 'I'm home' throw my
bag aside take off my clothes discard them say Goodnight
and climb

inside it

ただいまおやすみなさいオカエリただいまおかえりオヤスミナサイおかえりおかえり
誕生する
わたしのなかにはなにもない
壊れたら　こんどは一人だから台車がいるだろういつか粗大ゴミ置き場まで行く男の
誕生日には台車をプレゼントしておいてあげようおめでとう
ただいま　　肌は夜明けの青いいろ

\<squeak\>

He comes home, quietly seats himself on the sofa, and draining the
    can of beer he has opened, gazes

at me, sleeping

at the empty aquarium

or the blank screen of the no-longer-there broken television

head full of nothing

I'm home goodnight *welcome home* I'm home welcome home *goodnight*
    welcome home *welcome home*

Something is being born

I am full of nothing

When I get broken   this time he'll be on his own, perhaps he'll
    need a trolley, for the day he'll have to take me
    to the large waste drop-off

I'd better give him a trolley for a birthday present
    Happy Birthday!

I'm home   My skin is the blue colour of dawn

人造

湖は午後の日射しにぬるんでいる
手を離さないでいてね
スワンボートが浮かぶ水面は眠いから
ゆっくり歩くわたしは娘に繰り返し囁いた
それとも娘が歌うようにわたしに繰り返していたのだろうか
冷たい草の茎みたいな指先がそのたびにきゅっと震える
つながって震える
手を離さないでいて
遊歩道の向こうは小さなアミューズメントパーク
整えられた樹木に隠されてジェットコースターが
時折ゴオォォッ……と近づいては遠ざかり
聞こえてくる楽しげな悲鳴
反射的に指先に力がこめられて少しだけ爪がくいこむ
そう
そうしていてね
そうしていたはずなのに

Artificial

The lake is warming in the afternoon sunlight

Don't let go of my hand, OK?

There where the Swan Boat floats, the surface of the water is drowsy

I was walking slowly, murmuring this over and over to my daughter

or perhaps my daughter was sing-songing it over and over to me

Every time, her fingertips like stalks of cold grass give a little shiver

linked with my fingers   they shiver

Don't let go of my hand

On the other side of the promenade is a little amusement park

hidden among manicured shrubs. A jet coaster

swerves close and swings away at regular intervals, with a rising-
    fading RRRROOOOooaaaaaarrr

The sound of delighted shrieks carries to us

Instinctively she grips harder with her fingers and, just a little, her
    fingernails dig in

Yes, like that

Keep holding on like that, OK?

She was supposed to keep holding on like that

but before I know it, my daughter has disappeared

いつのまにか娘はいなくなった
遊歩道の敷石にソフトクリームの垂れ落ちた跡
どこへ行ったの
貸しボート屋の二階のレストハウスは閉まったまま
窓際に飾られた鮮やかな花は枯れることがない
つくられた湖を蓋するように磨りガラスめいた空が頭上を覆い
ゴオオォッ……と近づいては遠ざかる響き
悲鳴が消えていく
離れて
失われて
いない娘を求めてわたしは湖をめぐる
ここにないものを見つけようとする眼球は漣立ち
土産物屋に揺れる人影がどれも娘のような気がする
いいえ欲しいかどうかわからない何かを探しているあれはわたしなのか
どこにもいない
最初からいなかったのかもしれない
わたしの娘はどこにも
遠いスピーカーから流れる間延びしたメロディ

On the paving stones of the esplanade, a stain where an ice cream has melted and dripped

Where did you go to?

The public seating on the second floor of the rent-a-boat place is still closed

The vivid flowers decorating the windowsill never wither

The smoked-glass sky is coming down on top of our heads, as if closing the lid on the artificial lake

Echoes swerve close and swing away with a RRRROOOOooaaaaaarrr

The shrieks are fading

parted

lost

Hunting my daughter who is not here I circle the lake

searching for a thing not here, my eyeballs make ripples

Every one of the silhouettes flickering in the souvenir shop seems to be my daughter

No, perhaps that is me, searching for something I am not sure if I want or not

She isn't anywhere

It may be she was never here to begin with

My daughter, never anywhere

A slow melody slurring from a far-away speaker

最初からいなかった
わたしは娘を捨てたのだろうか
わたしはずっとひとりだったから
それとも娘がわたしを捨てたのだろうか
いらなくなって
どこへ行くこともできない
微かに吹き渡ってくる風は埃っぽくなつかしい肌に似たにおい
つくられた湖の縁に
そうだ娘だったのはわたしのほうで
つながれた手から離れてここまで来たのだったかもしれない
ゴオオォッ……
近づいて遠ざかる
娘はいない
遠ざかって近づく
娘はいる
わたしのなかに
つくられた湖
手を離さないでいてね
いなくなるから

She was never here to begin with

I wonder if I have thrown my daughter away

because I have always been on my own

Or perhaps my daughter has thrown me away

having no further use for me

You can never get to anywhere from the edge of the artificial lake

The breeze blowing faintly across toward me here has a dusty nostalgic
   scent, like skin

Now I see, maybe it was me who was the daughter,

who lost hold of linked fingers and found her way here

RRRROOOOooaaaaaarrr

swerving close and swinging away

my daughter is not here

swerving away and swinging close

my daughter is here

inside me

an artificial lake

Don't let go of my hand OK?

because you'll disappear

over and over

Even as they fade the shrieks reverberate

繰り返し

消えながら悲鳴は反響する
わたしのなかにいた
いたかもしれない何かがいなくなって
いなかったかもしれない何かのかたちが
明るい水になって広がっているこれは
わたしですか娘ですか娘のいないわたしはいますかここに
ないものを見つめようとする眼差しだけが残されて
まだ震えている指先の
うるおう草の先端に湛えられた水滴のような爪で
湖に触れる
失われたものもないものも
思い出せないものも忘れられないものもとけて混ざった水の肌に
しるすように少しだけくいこませて
つながれていく

She was inside me

A something, who may have been there, disappeared

A something, who may not have been there,

this thing, which has formed itself into bright water
  and is spreading out,

is it me, is it my daughter, me who has no daughter, am I here?

All that remains is a gaze, trying to fix on a thing not there

The still-shivering fingertips,

with fingernails like water droplets swelling on the tips of damp grass

touch the lake

Things that have been lost and things that are not there,

things I can't recall and things I can't forget, melted and mixed, into
  the skin of the water

digging in, just a little, to leave a mark

tangled together like fingers

夏の果は血のように滴る

父は夏に死にました

もうずいぶん前のことです

そのときわたしは日盛りの暑さで頭がわれるように痛いと思いながら

遠く離れた東京の街路をなにも知らずに歩いていて

携帯電話なんかまだ誰も持ってなくて

夜になって帰宅してから伝言を聞いて折り返し電話をかけたら

母はわたしの名を呼んで「かなしい」とだけ言いましたたぶん泣きながら

翌日の早朝に弟と東京駅でおちあい四時間半かけて小浜へ

帰り着いたらやっぱりひどい暑さでした

集まった親戚や近所のひとたちで狭い家はざわついていて

誰かが茹でておいてくれた素麺をさあ食べて一息つきなさいと台所の隅で出されたけれど

味がしなくてそういえばわたしはそれから何年ものあいだ素麺を食べたくなくなった

凹のかたちに抱かれた海のある町で父はずっと電気工事の仕事をしていて

その夏の真昼　頭上に落下してきたものがあったのでした

ちょうど休憩時間になりヘルメットをとって汗を拭いながら歩き出したときでした

単純にいえばそういうこと

The Fruit of Summer Drips like Blood

My father died in summer

It's already a long time ago now

At the moment he died, I was thinking my head hurt so much from
   the heat of the full noon sun it was about to split

I was far away, walking the Tokyo streets, knowing nothing at all

(it's not like anyone had mobile phones yet)

That night, when I got home, I listened to my messages, made a
   return call,

my mother said my name then just 'It's sad' nothing more sounded
   like she was crying

Next day, early morning, I met up with my little brother at Tokyo
   station and we rode the four and a half hours back to Obama

When we got home, of course the heat was terrible

The tiny house noisy with gathered relatives and neighbours

Set out in the corner of the kitchen were some *sōmen* noodles someone
   had boiled up ready: 'there, eat, rest yourselves a moment'

but I couldn't taste them from then on I don't know how many years
   it was I couldn't eat *sōmen*

In this town on the sea, nestled in the hollow of the hills, my father
   worked his whole life as an electrical engineer

That high summer noon   something fell and struck him
   on top of his head.

もう少しこみいったことは何日かたってから父の会社の会議室で説明され

ああ事故って起こるんだなと思いました

どの一人が悪いっていうんじゃなく人間が集まってやっていることだから事故は起こる

どこでだって

二人は仲が良かったから母はおそろしいくらいに泣き

いっしょにいくのだと棺にとりすがるので

母の姉とわたしは監視するみたいに母から離れないようにして二日間を過ごし

ようやくひとの少なくなった家の不思議にあかるい台所で

夥しい数のコップや皿を三人で黙々と洗ったのは

通夜も葬式も終わってからのこと

母が突然「キーホルダーがない」と言い出しました

なんのことかわからずに伯母とわたしは顔を見あわせましたが

母は小走りに勝手口から出て行きくちをかたく結んで裏に置いてあったゴミ袋を

持って戻ってくると三和土でそのくちをほどきました

冬にいっしょに温泉へ出かけた（それが二人の最後の旅行になった）

記念に買って財布かなにかに付けて肌身離さず持っていたはずのそれが

病院から渡された携行品のなかにはなかったと

It had just gone break time. He had taken off his helmet and was
    wiping the sweat away as he started to walk off

That's the simple version

We got a slightly more complicated version a few days later,
    in the meeting room at my father's company

I thought, oh. Accidents really do happen

Not to say any one person was in the wrong, but this is humans doing
    things as a group, so accidents will happen

Anywhere, to anyone

Because the two of them cared for each other, my mother cried
    terribly,

and because she clung to the coffin, saying, I'm going with him,

my mother's elder sister and I spent two days without leaving
    her side, as if we had placed her under surveillance

At last, in the emptied-out house, in the strangely bright kitchen

when the three of us were absorbed in washing up innumerable cups
    and plates

(this was after the wake, after the funeral)

my mother burst out: 'The key-ring is missing!'

Not knowing what she was talking about, my aunt and I exchanged
    glances, but

my mother trotted out the back door to the garbage bag, which
    had been tied firmly and put out behind the house, picked it up,
    brought it back inside

母は言いつのります
ゴミ袋のなかにあったとき父が着ていた作業着が入っていて
大量の血が染みこんだ布は真夏の二日を経てほどかれてすさまじいにおいを放ちました
漁港と魚市場のある町で育ったけれどこんなにおいはかいだことがない
わたしのなかをいま流れているものにとても近いはずの血が
生きている体から流れ出てしまえばこんなになるのだと
呆然としながら息をとめて
いつもてきぱきしていておしゃべりな伯母も無言のまま動かず
母だけが話し続けながら（だから息をとめることもなく）
ゴミ袋に両手をつっこんですっかり色の変わった作業着を広げ
内ポケットの底にあったキーホルダーを素手でさぐりあてて取り出しました
「ほら、あった」と幸福そうに笑っているこのひととは
誰なのだろう
病的なほどきれい好きで神経質で気が小さく
肉も生魚も苦手だから料理のためにさわるのも本当は嫌だと言ったあの母じゃない
獣のように血のにおいのなかで微笑んでいる
わたしはこのひとを知らない
濃い夏の夕暮れ深く

Once she was on the packed dirt in the little space next to the kitchen, she untied it

'In winter, we went to a hot-spring together' (it ended up being their last trip together)

'He bought it as a memento, and he never parted from it, he should have had it with him, attached to his wallet or something, but

it wasn't with the personal effects the hospital returned to us'

insists my mother

Inside the garbage bag was the work uniform my father was wearing at the time of the accident

It was two full-summer days since large quantities of blood had soaked into the fabric—unwrapped, it gave off a dreadful smell

I grew up in a harbour town with fish markets but I have never smelt a smell like it

This blood, which should be very close to what is now flowing inside me,

this is what it becomes when it all drains out of a living body

I thought, in blank amazement, and held my breath

My aunt too, my always-bustling, always-chattering aunt, stayed mute and stock still

Only my mother was able to keep talking (which meant also she was still breathing in)

She shoved both her hands into the garbage bag, spreading out the work uniform which had completely changed colour with blood

With her bare hands, rooting around, she found the key-ring at the bottom of the inside pocket, and pulled it out

かろうじて左右の口角を吊りあげてうなずいたわたしは
おそらく生まれて初めて
たった一度だけ母を
畏怖しました

（血は流れた
血は流れている
わたしのそとに
わたしのなかに
わたしかもしれない獣がそこにいて
どこへも届かない遠吠えを滴らせている）

夏に死んだ父には
いろいろなところから瑞々しい果物が届けられ供えられました
葡萄　バナナ　桃　梨　メロン　葡萄　桃　桃　蜜柑　西瓜　梨
仏壇から漂うあまいにおいはまたたくまにねっとりと濃くなり
すぐに黒いこまかな虫が飛び始める
母とわたしは追われるように

laughing joyfully 'ah, there it is!'

Who is this person?

It isn't that mother, abnormally neat, nervous and timid, so unable
   to deal with meat and raw fish, she hated to touch them
   even for cooking.

She is grinning like a beast in the midst of the stench of blood

I do not know this person

In the depths of the saturated summer twilight

I nodded, barely managing to turn up the left and right corners
   of my mouth

I dare say it is the one and only time in my life

I have stood in awe of my mother

   blood flowed

   blood is flowing

   outside me

   inside me

   a beast which might be me is right there

   letting drip a howling that no one can hear

To my father who died in the summertime

from all sorts of places, pieces of luscious fruit were delivered and
   laid out as offerings

毎日まいにち腐ってゆく順番に果物を切り皮をむき
食べ続けました
すべてが終わってしんとなった家で
噛みしめるまもなくとけ崩れていく果肉の汁が指から腕へ幾筋もつたって
おいしいかどうかもはやわからない滴を唇から胸元まであふれこぼれさせてすすりこむ
暑い夏でした

grapes bananas peaches pears melons grapes peaches peaches
mandarins watermelons pears

the sweet smell wafting from the family altar becoming in no time
sticky and cloying

and soon after, tiny black insects beginning to cloud the air

My mother and I, as if driven,

day after day, took the fruit in order as it was about to go bad,
cut it, peeled off its skin

and kept eating

in the silent house, everything over,

the fruit flesh melting and coming apart as soon as we bit into it, the
juice dripping from our fingers, our arms, in a network of veins

already not knowing if it was delicious or not, we drooled it from our
lips to our breastbones, slurping it noisily back into our mouths

That was a hot summer

KONO SATOKO
河野聡子

translated by

SHANE STRANGE

シェーン・ストレンジ

&

RINA KIKUCHI

菊地利奈

専用

骨の枠で頭がしめつけられてつらい。

骨を切ってぼくをとりだしてほしい。

ある朝ぼくの首がそういったきり、キャビネットから出てこなくなった

月曜日専用の首である

ついにきたか

火曜、水曜、木曜、金曜の首はつぶやいたが、土曜と日曜の首は寝ていた

近年首のひきこもりは社会問題になっている

ぼくの首は7つしかない

たった7つの首で、月曜から日曜までの7日間を切り回している

ぼくらは生まれたときからキャビネットを持っている

標準仕様のキャビネットは扉が6つあり、それぞれちがう首が入っている

毎日ちがう首で学校へ来なさい、

適切な時と場合に適切な首を選びなさい、さもないと

このように毎日首のちがう教師はぼくらを脅したものだった。

Head Ache

'My skull's being squeezed,

cut the bone, take me out!'

This was Monday head.

'I knew this was coming,'

mumbled Tuesday, Wednesday, Thursday, and Friday heads.

Saturday and Sunday heads were asleep.

Managing heads is becoming a problem,

with only seven

to last the week.

They have lived in the closet since the day I was born.

A closet with six doors. Behind each door, a different head.

At school, teachers said:

'Come to school each day with a different head.'

'Choose the right head, or else…'

Creative head was for the day of art class;

Physical head for playing dodge ball;

Maths head excelled at calculation.

器用な首は美術の日に、体育が得意な首はドッチボールの日に、計算が得意な首は算数の日に。

おしゃべりな首、根気のある首、喧嘩っ早い首、泣き虫の首、見栄っ張りの首

今日はどの首にしようか

これを曜日で決める同僚は気楽で、気分で変える上司は最悪である

とはいえぼくの上司もかつては気楽な上司だった、ところが

「人間としておもしろい」のは首を気分で変える者

なる調査結果が発表され、上司は首をランダムに変えるようになった

月曜の首は変化と予測不可能な現象が苦手だった

月曜の首はいちばん頭がよかった

月曜の首はさっさと絶望した

月曜の首がひきこもりになったのも無理はなかった

月曜ほど頭のよくない残りのぼくらは途方にくれ

いまキャビネット越しに口論しているところだ

月曜の首当番をジャンケンで決めろというのか

ジャンケン、

首には手も指もない

何度やっても土曜の首が後出しするため、口ジャンケンは中止になった

Chatty head, stubborn head, pushy head, sooky head, stuck-up
head—

How can I get my heads together?

A care-free colleague said use the days of the week.

Bad bosses choose their heads by their mood.

My boss used to be care-free, until he read an article:

'Impressive People Choose Their Heads by Mood'.

He changed his head accordingly. It did no good.

Monday head—the cleverest head—

can no longer cope with the world as it is

and so has abandoned all hope.

I can understand this, I guess.

'We, the rest of the heads, who are not as clever as Monday
head, are bewildered.'

They argue through the closet doors.

'Are we meant to decide who will take Monday's place by
playing 'scissors, paper, rock'?

むかしの人にとっては、顔の美醜が大きな問題だったそうだ
少なくともひとつは首についている顔ごときが、どうして問題だったのか
まるで夢物語のようだ
明日は月曜日で、首問題は未解決である
こうしてぼくも「人間としておもしろく」なっていくらしい

Heads don't have fingers or hands!'

They try a talking version:

'Sci-ssors, pa-per, rock!'

Saturday head cheats every time.

Tomorrow will be Monday, and the head problem remains unsolved.

Once upon a time, it was important to present a beautiful face to the world.

But now, with each head having one face,

it is more important to choose the right head.

I will just have to choose my head

like a boss.

エアロバイク洗濯マシーン

全世界の男女が美容とダイエットにかける情熱、深夜のテレビ番組でダンベルや得体のしれないプラスチック製の器械を買いこむ人々のことを考えてみてください。代替エネルギーとして求められるのは、この情熱をエネルギーへと変換し、ダイエットを完遂させ見栄をみたし運動不足も解決し将来の成人病に備えながら日々の生活に必要な家事さえ行うという一石五鳥ともいえる仕組みです。これを実現させるのがエアロバイク洗濯マシーンです。バイクをこぐこと、それはすなわち洗濯をすることであり、運動をすることであり、健康に配慮することです。スポーツジムにもエアロバイクがずらりとならび、人々は壁や窓にむかってひたすらこぎ続けると同時に、コインランドリーの使用権も手に入れます。

Proposals for New Forms of Alternative Energy: Spin Cycle

Think about men and women the world over who are obsessed by beauty and diet—people who buy weights and useless plastic machines on TV shopping channels in the middle of the night. Have you ever wondered how we could harness this obsession? What if we could stop the useless diets, look good, get healthier and reduce the risk of preventable disease, all while doing the daily chores? Introducing 'Spin Cycle': a combination exercise bike and washing machine. Cycle through your washing while getting healthy and saving the planet. Have you seen the stationary cycles lined up in a row at the gym, with people pedalling forever staring at the wall or out the window? They're getting nowhere! 'Spin Cycle'—pedal your way to good health *and* do the laundry.

靴

靴こそは、人間の力が無意識にふるわれている最たるものです。毎日の生活に欠かせず、歩くたびに何らかの力を受け、くたびれ、しいたげられているが、けっして文句をいわず、雨にも負けず、風にも負けず、雪にも、夏の歩道の暑さにも耐え、穴があいても踵が取れても、ぐちひとつ言わず外科手術に耐え、小石や泥の道でも従順に人間の足を守り従っているのです。その彼らが発電もできるとなったら！　人間はついに靴に頭があがらなくなり、上ではなく下にあるものこそが偉大なものとなり、それでも靴はけっしておごりたかぶらず、そういうものに私はなりたい、などということもない。こんな謙虚な靴たちが、いまやぞくぞくと歩き出そうとしています。

Proposals for New Forms of Alternative Energy: Shoe Power

Look at shoes. Why do we ignore them? What power we are wasting! Shoes are necessary in daily life. Every time we walk, they make power. Shoes get tired and they are humiliated. Despite this, they never complain. They stand strong in rain. They stand strong in wind. They stand strong in snow. They endure the heat of the pavement in summer. They don't even grumble when they are worn through, or when their heels come off and they have to have surgery. They protect the feet of human kind so obediently—even on the muddy path; even on the gravel road. What if this power could produce electricity? Finally we would bow down to them. Those who are at the bottom will rise. Shoes would not brag, but remain humble. They would never say 'I want to be *all that*.' Now these humble shoes arise, taking their first steps, marching towards us, marching in the same direction.

MISAKI TAKAKO
岬多可子

translated by

SUBHASH JAIRETH
サバシュ・ジャイレス
&
RINA KIKUCHI
菊地利奈

白い闇のほうへ

うすくらがりは　うすあかるみ
仄見えていたものが　見えなくなり
見えなかったものが　仄見えてくる
そこへ　どこまでも　入っていけばいい
ぐったりとした　自分の重さを
たったひとつの　持ち物のように　ひきずって

かなしみの　白い布は
くるしみの　白い布は
一面にひろげられてあるだろう
これ以上　失えないほど　失って
そのあと　なにもかもが　白く
白く　そして　暗く

目も　手も　おぼつかない
しずかな　闇のなかで

178　　岬多可子

Into White Darkness

Barely dark   is barely light

all that was visible   has turned invisible

and the invisible   has come to light

there   however deep it is   we should go

exhausted   carrying the weight

of nothing   but our own bodies   dragged alongside

Of sorrow   the white shroud

of pain   the white shroud

stretched   across   the whole field

nothing   more   to lose

now   all is white   and more

white   and yet   strange darkness

Neither eyes   nor hands know   the way

in the   still darkness

only the heart   has its work

we sort   as if   beans from the gravel

できるのは　こころの仕事
砂利と　豆を　たんねんによりわけるように
つまずきを　つまずきながらかぞえるように
ゆっくりと　ゆっくりと

祈るとき　悼むとき　わたくしたち
ひとりずつ立ち　それぞれの
もっとも深いところへ向けて　うつむく
片方の手は　もう片方の手を
あるいは　どこかにあるはずの
見知らぬ　熱い手を　求める

吐かれた息　流された涙が
白い闇を　あたためる
ほつほつと　筆の先の色がにじむように
小さな炎は点され
やがて　まじりあって　大きくかがやく
そのときまで　そこに　とどまっていればいい

stumble   count our stumbles

slowly   so slowly

We pray   we grieve

we stand   next to each other

but alone   heads lowered   bodies curled

and hands   stretched out   looking for

other hands   to rescue   to hold

to farewell   to mourn   and remember

We exhale   we cry

warming   the white darkness   with breath and tears

as if   daubing it   with colours

dropped   from the paintbrush

and making it   glow   like embers   around us

as   we wait   still   silent   becalmed

琉金

まるまると　ひら　びら　と
行き交う　金魚の上を
歩いていかねばならないのが

まして　今日は
こんなに尖った靴を履いているので
とても　ほんとうは　こわい

罪の深さに　底などないが
胴体を　朱に金に
まんまんと　ふくらませて
ひしめいているのが
きっと　その量

どれだけの　もの　こと　を
傷つけてきたか

The Goldfish

Stout and stubby   they swish and swoosh

the gold fish   swim under my feet

as I walk on top

But today   more than ever

in my sharp pencil-heel shoes

I feel   horribly   scared

We are   endlessly cruel

the fish are aureate and crimson

fleshy and   puffed

swarming the place

like our own   acts of inequity

How much life have we destroyed

and how long will this continue?

They razzle and dazzle   playing with the light

squirming and turning

きらぎらと　光を散らすように
泳いでいる　流れているのを
赤い河みたいに思って
どんなに気をつけても　また　つぎを
つぎも　踏んでしまう

逆流するようで　血の
とどこおり　泡だつ　あたり
とろけた春の藻が
細い踵に　からみつく

forming a red river

I hesitate   take care and yet

I still step on this one and that

The blood trickles

doesn't flow and drops thicken

staining the spring weed that

twists and twines   around my spiky heels

MISUMI MIZUKI
三角みづ紀

translated by

NILOOFAR FANAIYAN

ニルーファー・ファナイヤン

&

RINA KIKUCHI

菊地利奈

プレゼント

今朝は
足首が見つからんから
あなたのもとへ、
行かれない。

それはひどく大変なことだ
いまから新しい足首を届けに行くよ。

恋人はすんなりと
わたしの
出来の悪い嘘を信じた
受話器を置いて
わたしは慌てて
出刃包丁で
足首を切断せんといかんかった
血がだくだく流れて
傷口と
こころが
しくしく痛んだ

188　三角みづ紀

The Gift

This morning
I cannot find my foot.
To you, to your abode,
I cannot come.

> *I am truly troubled by this news.*
> *I will bring you a new foot now.*

My beloved believed,
my   bad lie was believed—
I put the receiver down
and hastened
by broad-bladed carving knife
to remove my foot.
Blood pumped forth in gushing streams from the newly severed limb
        and my heart ached.

Yesterday,
for the first time, I cut my arm

昨日、
はじめて腕を切った
剃刃で浅く
ほんに浅く
傷をつけた
長い長い二本の裂け目から
わたしが零れてしまった
血液を吸い込んだ
ハンケチは
わたし自身
捨てられんかった

あなたはきっと
多分
いや
多分悲しむから
会いたくなかって、
会いたくなかった

足首を切断してから

with a razor—it was a fine cut, shallow—

very thinly

I made two wounds,

and from the two long long crevices, from those wounds,

I was spilling,   my blood was spilling,

and absorbing that blood—

the handkerchief—was

          myself.

I could not throw it away.

You, beloved, will perhaps,

will more likely,

no—

truly you will be very sad.

          I didn't want to see you.

                    I did not want to see you.

Three breaths after I removed my foot

the house bell rang,

and into the cupboard beneath the kitchen sink

I carelessly threw my foot.

三呼吸目にチャイムがなった
流しの下に
足首をほおりこむ

あまりにも早く
恋人は来た
あまりにも、
早すぎた

もしかしたら
あなたは本当は
おらんひとなのかもしれん

疑ってしまうのだ
恋人は
水色と緑色の混じった
きれいな足首をわたしに差し出した
土盛海岸の色
の足首

真っ白で長い

Too soon

my beloved came,

impossibly

soon.

I question if, perhaps,

it is you, actually,

you who is non-existent, not real.

I can't help myself, stop myself, from questioning

my beloved—

he presents to me a swirling marbled thing

of blue and turquoise,

the colours of pristine coastal waters—

my beautiful new foot.

So pure white and long

is my beloved's left arm—

there are two fine scars,

gruesome in their freshness, crimson lines.

恋人の左腕に
細い二本の傷
生々しい赤の線

わたし、
間違ってあなたの腕を切ったのだ

なんてことだ
わたし、

恋人は一言も発さず
手馴れた具合で
わたしに
足首をつけよった
浅い海のなかに居るように心細い
ひんやりとした
くるぶしまでの海

もしかしたら
わたしは本当は
おらんひとなのかもしれん
疑ってしまうのだ

Oh how has this horror happened?

I   have mistakenly cut your arm.

My beloved says not one word,

but with skilful fingers

attaches the new foot

to my severed limb.

I feel unsteady as though standing in shallow waters—

a cool sensation

as the seawater laps up and past my ankle.

I question if, perhaps,

it is I, actually,

myself who is non-existent, not real.

Afterwards, on the kitchen floor,

we lost our original forms—

      we didn't keep ourselves—

          we did not keep ourselves.

台所の床の上で
乱暴なセックスをしたら
わたしたち
もう原形をとどめて
いなかって、
いなかった

それでもお腹はすく
朝食を作りましょうよ
曖昧な生き物のまま
わたしは立ち上がった
相変わらず
足首は土盛海岸に居る

わたし
もう傷なんてつけん
あなたまで切りつけてしまうから
だから
もう、せんよ

恋人は未だ

Despite this shift in form we felt hungry,

we made breakfast,

as ghost-like and ambiguous creatures—

I stood up

and, as before,

my foot remained on the Tsuchimori coast.

No longer will I scar myself, never again—

because I would be scarring you,

that is why—

never again.

My beloved still

has not spoken a word—

smiling,

he turns into a small cuddly pig.

We,

in reality,

may be non-existent, not real.

一言も発さず
微笑んで
小さな豚になった

わたしたち
本当は
おらんひとなのかもしれんけど
それでも
このひとが大好きだ
その事実にこころを殴られ
わたしは
不覚にも
泣いてしまう

Even so,

I love this person—

my heart is hammering with this love.

And despite myself,

I am weeping.

洗濯機

日常ですきなのは
洗濯をすること
雨降りの日でも
真夜中でも
かまわず洗濯をする

シャツとタオルと下着と靴下
泡たてて　きれいになるから
自分まで　きれいになる心地
仕上がる前の　加速するあの音
飛行機が離陸する音に似ている

ふたりぶんの
衣類と一緒に
わたしたちを
丁寧に干した

Washing Machine—Berlin, 2016

my favourite thing

is doing the washing;

even when it rains,

even at midnight—

I do the washing despite it all

shirts and towels and underwear and socks

watching the rotating bubbles and soap suds

watching the cleaning   I am becoming clean

that accelerating noise just before the spinning stops—

that sound that resembles the sound of an aeroplane taking off

we are

two lots

of freshly washed clothes, so precious,

being carefully draped over hangers   hangers carefully hung on
    the clothes line

drying   sunbathing in fresh air

清潔になって
並んでいたら
すべてうまくいく気がする

たたむのは苦手だから
ハンガーに干されて
きれいなままで
空に浮いていたい

becoming   and finding   inner and outer
spotlessness

beside each other—

everything is going to be fine

I am not good at folding

so I leave everything hanging   drying on the hangers

forever clean and free—

I want to float in the sky

市場

快晴の昼下がりに
地下鉄に揺られて
たくさんはいるバッグを持って
市場へ向かう

ひとつきだけの
わたしの暮らし
まもなくおしまいだから
チーズやハムは　あきらめて
パンとすこしの野菜を求める
あたたかくなっても使えそうなストールと
スーツケースにほうりこむラベンダー袋も

ないものねだり。
ずっと　こんな生活が
続けばよいのだけれど
わたしはただの通過者
人生のはじまりとおわりを

The Market—Berlin, 2016

A sunny, blue, cloudless sky.

Just after midday, being shaken by the subway,

carrying a magic satchel,

I head to the market.

After only one month

this life

is ending

and I am giving up cheese and ham—

I buy bread and a few vegetables,

a light shawl to use in warmer weather,

a lavender sachet to throw in my suitcase.

'You always want what you can't have'—

longer,   forever,   a life like this—

I wish it could last

but I am only a passenger.

It is difficult

自分で決めるのは
むずかしいが
旅であったら
はじまりとおわりを
決めることができる

生まれて、死ぬこと
はじまり、おわること

幾度となく
生まれ変わるために
わたしは
わたしの町ではない町を進む

死んだものと生きるものが並んでいる
市場の片隅の
花屋の花々に心をうばわれるが
枯れるのを見届けられないから
買わずに
帰る

to decide by yourself

the beginnings and endings of life,

but if it is all a series of journeys,

then you can decide

the starts and ends of the journeys.

Being born   Dying

Beginning   Ending

Countlessly

to be reborn,

I   proceed, marching through the town which is not my own.

Dead things and living things are arranged next to each other

in a corner of the market—

my heart is stolen by the flowers in that corner,

but I cannot bring myself to watch over the withering of flowers

so without buying

I leave.

NAKAMURA SACHIKO
中村祥子

translated by

CASSANDRA ATHERTON
カッサンドラ・アサトン

&

RINA KIKUCHI
菊地利奈

まぶしい朝が来て

父親を看取ったあとの放心なのか
長い介護の疲れなのか
無事でいることの罪悪感か
高台の病室から
それを見ていた天罰か

霊安室は満杯です棺は被災者様の分です●が押さえているのでどこに行っても一般の方にはあそこ見てすごい煙よ迂回路なし火事じゃないのかこの先通行止だれか消防車を家族が見つからないんです尋ね人はここにご記入ください急げ消防署まで走れ走れ火葬は順番待ちです担当が呼びに行くまでお待ちください

並んでも並んでも
衛星電話はつながらない

下着と交換で水を分けてください遺体袋しかもらえなかったよ商品は一人三個までガソリンは十リッターまで今から一時間後に火葬ですあれっ棺に入れないと火葬できませんベニ

And the Bright Morning Comes

Is this the hollowness of my father's death?

Or the bone tiredness of his long illness in my chest?

From the hospital window, I watched it unfold.

Is this emptiness the heavy guilt of inaction?

Or punishment for surviving?

crematoria are overflowing there are no more coffins ● *is to blame they control the living and the dead look there are huge smoke clouds rising No Detour Isn't that fire? Road Closed call the fire brigade we can't find our family please write down the names of the people you have lost hurry run to the fire station wait in line for the cremation of your loved ones we will call your name when it's your turn*

Waiting waiting

The satellite calls cannot be connected

please would you swap your spare underwear for some water? oh no, only plastic bags Limit Of Up To 3 Items Limit Of Up To 10 Litres Of Petrol we will be cremating your family member in one hour oh! the body must be in a coffin use this chipboard please hurry up people are waiting but can't you

ヤ板ならありますが次の方がお待ちです早く何とかして袋に入れたり出したりかわいそう
ね急いでくださいー本の花も見つからなくてでは合掌願います良かったわね病気で死んで

ほろりと崩れる父の遺骨は
ほとんどが灰で
全部すくって白い袋に納める
それから検死が済んだとの知らせがきて
三人並べて伯母一家の火葬がある

ひどい傷だな三人とも玄関で重なり合っていたそうよ結構集まりましたねお花をどうぞ姉
さん痛かったでしょうになんてきれいな骨だことこんなに白くてつやつやして
三つとも違う入れ物だぞ仕方ないじゃないの

四十九日目にやっと兄弟がそろって
それぞれが被災していたことを知る

沿岸への道はすべて閉鎖されていた通してくださいお願いします父が危篤で今夜が山なん
ですそんなことを言ってもだめです嘘じゃないできるもんなら病院にいる妹に電話してく

do something? it's too sad to keep moving his body in and out of this bag just hurry up but we wanted to have flowers and we can't find even one now let's pray he is lucky to have died from his illness

My father's bones shrink to fragments and ash;

I scoop up everything, every bit of bone dust and place it in a small
  white bag.

My great aunt and her family are next to be cremated.

I did not know they were victims.

terrible scars three bodies huddled together on the front porch relatives have gathered please take a flower my older sister you must have suffered greatly it's time how beautifully white and smooth their bones are but these urns don't match I'm sorry there is nothing we can do

Forty-nine days after my father's death,

I reunite with my brothers; we are all broken

all the coastline roads are blocked please let me pass I beg you please my father is on the cusp of death tonight no I can't trust this you can call my sister who is there no I cannot let you go there is nothing but a dangerous wasteland of brokenness please just give in I'm telling you this for your own good

れ道路が決壊していて通れませんあなたのために言っているんだもうあきらめてください

警察官だってくたくただったろうに
兄がそう締めくくったあとで
おれは地獄を見たよ。と弟がうつむく

気がつくと周りは海だった孤立した会社の窓から一晩中消火ホースを伸ばしていたんだ助
ケテクレーどこだー助ケテクレー真っ暗で何も見えなかった助ケテー助ケテ気がついた
ら隣にカメラを持った変な男がいる何だお前はうるさいこっちも命がけで取材してるんだ
馬鹿野郎こんな時に邪魔だけどけど助ケテクレー助ケテエあっちからもこっちからも
そっちからもおーい頑張れーオーイコッチダ助ケテクレー朝までは確かに聞こえていたん
だダレカ助ケテダレカ頑張れえ頑張れええ

弟はあの日から心を病んで
兄は私にも病院へ行けと言う
でもウツの薬はずっと処方されている

That policeman must have been dead tired

was the last line my older brother uttered

My younger brother bowed his head and said I saw hell that night

when I looked out of the window of the company building all I could see was ocean I could hear people calling all night I stretched the fire extinguisher's hose hoping to reach someone help where are you? help me it was pitch dark I could see nothing suddenly what? what are you doing? shut up I'm reporting I'm risking my life to record the truth you are in the way. I could hear so many calls HELP where are you? HELP ME OVER HERE hello SOMEONE HELP ME hang on THIS WAY I'm coming I NEED ASSISTANCE hold on HELP where are you? hang ooooooooooonnnnnnn surely those cries were heard till morning

His illness surges in him.

My older brother wants to save me from

the same fate, but I am already in therapy.

You have been through so much.

I suffered, but so did you.

なんだかいっぺんに老けたな
お互いさまじゃないの

語ろうあの日の海を語ろう生きているこの奇跡を語ろうあのどうしようもない闇の深さを
語ろうひたすらに前を向く日々を語らないと

まるで当たり前のように
きょうも
まぶしい朝が来て

let's talk about the sea we saw that day let's talk about why we survived let's talk about the unspeakable darkness about the days we have to live after all that we have loved is gone we must talk we have to talk

Nothing can be the same

but a new day still dawns

and the bright morning comes.

中村祥子

YAMASAKI KAYOKO
山崎佳代子

translated by

SUBHASH JAIRETH
サバシュ・ジャイレス
&
RINA KIKUCHI
菊地利奈

砂時計

さらさらと落ちてゆく　私たちは砂だ
形状、重量ともに均質　色はどれも鳩の
かぼそい足の　薄紅色だ

天国と地獄は　透きとおったガラスの
皮膜に被われて　形よい身体の中央に
作られた窪みで　隔てられている

さらさらと落ちてゆき　最後の砂が
窪みを　滑り落ちてしまうと　命のない
空っぽの天国が残る

その瞬間に　診療室は緊張する
私たちの下降に意味があるのはその時だけだ
地獄に留まった後の　私たちの沈黙に

The Hour-glass

soft, like so it falls   we are but sand

grains as light or heavy   coloured

pale red   of a pigeon's scrawny leg

the heaven the hell   are both glass

see-through   shapely and in the middle

a pinched neck separating the bulbs

soft, like so   drops the last grain

through the neck leaving the

heaven empty   hollow alone

meanwhile   in the surgery the air

is edgy   we have meaning only when we flow

to stop is hell   hushed and silent

oblivious   the hour-glass

in the surgery gathers dust

the silence floats through the seasons but

もう　だれも興味をしめさない
室に漂う埃を被って
長い沈黙が続く季節もあるが

再び　あの男が降り向いて
器を覆すと、一度に　天国と地獄が
逆さになって

さらさらと　私たちは、限られた天国の
時間を刻み始める　ガラスの中に
閉ざされた地獄への　落下時間を
さらさらと落ちてゆく　私たちは砂だ

then   the surgeon's hand turns over

the hour-glass just like that   reversing

the heaven and the hell

soft, like so   we fall again

the time ticks in the hour-glass

to lodge us in hell   the time drops

soft, like so, we fall   the grains of sand.

木

しらぬまに異郷で　私は木になっていた
鳥も巣を掛けず実も葉もつけぬから
私には名前がない

黒緑の皮に覆われ顔を失ったが
国境の噂を聞くばかり
血のまじる雲間を旋回する鳥に

男に枝を一本払われ　傷は瞳になった
残る一本の枝で雲を払いのけようと
悶えるばかり

次に　男が村に来る日
根元から切り倒されるだろう
私のマルタが乾かぬうちに

Tree

unbeknown to me I became a tree   in this alien land
a tree without a nest for birds, without fruits or leaves
I remain uncalled unnamed

over me hang the blood-stained clouds and a raven lost in flight
I hear only rumours of the happenings at the borders
my skin has blackened, my face is disfigured but then

a man hacks off a branch   leaving a scar shaped like an eye
now I have but one branch with which I fend off clouds
it hurts each time I swing the branch

soon   the man will return
to slash at my roots and grind my stump
and before it has even dried

the village carpenter   will measure a casket for a soldier
his body still warm neatly placed inside
the lid nailed and the body engulfed by my wooden embrace

職人に　兵士を葬る棺を作らせ
釘を打たせ蓋をさせる
私の板はまだ温かい頑丈な体を抱かされ

地に埋められ
私の木切れは　村人の肢体と一緒に
穴に投げ込まれ火を放たれ

私の木屑は灰になり
雲を舞い　泣くだろう
部隊は正しい呼吸のように村を訪れ

少女の臀部がやっと乗るほどの
私の切り株に
鶏の首が乗せられると

鉈は振り下ろされ
草原を首なし鶏が跳ね回る
肩の小さな少年も捕えられ

interned in the ground we'll remain

when the remnants   of wood and the body

will be gathered in a hall and set alight

the wood will turn into ashes

twirling with the clouds   weeping and wailing

meanwhile soldiers marching in step will enter the village again

and on my sliced stump barely

the size of a little girl's

soft buttock the heads of chooks will be placed

the hatchet will swing down

again and again and I'll see headless chooks hopping in the field

and amongst them a little boy of slender shoulders

his head donned with silky chestnut hair too will find a place

on the stump and the hatchet will swing down

drowning the cries of his sister as her ashen-faced mother will collapse

柔らかな栗毛の頭が乗せられ
鉈が振り下ろされる
妹が泣きじゃくり母が気絶しても

男は腹を抱え笑い声をたて
油じみた熱い目を潤ませ
女たちの体を鍋に投げ入れ

酒を食らうばかりだ
私の切り株は血に染まるだろう
鳥が肉の気配に舞い降りる

こびりついた血のせいで
年輪が読み取れない
切り株には待つことだけが許される

水盤となる朝を
雨に満たされた水面が
鳥の影を映す朝を

but the man, now dressed as a soldier, his hands on his hips

will roar a shameless laugh   his reddened eyes watering
    from the effort

before he will throw her and other dead women in his devil's

cauldron and will drink and drink as my stump

will be drenched in blood of the dead and then

the raven will descend to land near the stump smelling of flesh

and look at the trunk soaked with blood

unable to read in the smeared rings my age

and so I'll wait, the chopped down trunk of a tree

wait for the morning to turn into a stoup

filled to the brim with rain water

wishing for the raven to come look and leave its fleeting image.

一時帰国

家々のたたずまい
人々の立ち居ふるまい
それをただ眺めていたかった

母語のどよめき
声と声の重なりあい
午後の電車が乗せて走る
人々のざわめき
どんより疲れた顔、はずんだ表情
秋のおわりの黄金色や紅色
光と影のまじわりに
酩酊し

祭りの晩
風の盆おどりを
訪ねてやって来た

Coming Home for a Brief Visit

House after house

Face after face

I want to look and look

Hearing my mother's tongue

I'm baffled by the cacophony

In the afternoon train

I see a restless crowd

some appear tired others cheery

the autumn outside is amber and red

a play of light and shadows

dazed I feel dizzy

In the evening

at the bon-matsuri

I feel like a stranger

on a visit

alone

unable to join

旅の人のように
みずからは
踊らず歌わず
踊りの輪を
遠くから
眺めるように

通りすがりの者の眼で
私は見つめる
私のものでありながら
もはや私のもの
ではない
母の国
の表情を

the dancers in the circle

as I watch

from a distance

like a passer-by

I gaze

at the face

of my motherland

mine and yet

nevermore

mine.

TRANSLATORS'
NOTES

The Japanese naming convention of family name followed by a given name has been used for the Japanese poets throughout this book.

A Lightbulb

The male voice in this poem's dialogue is written in Tohoku dialect, while the woman's is standardised Japanese, as spoken in Tokyo.

Tsubaki is a single-layered winter camellia, usually deep red or pure white. The flower is associated with traveling courtesans, who carried it both as a medicinal remedy and to indicate their profession. There is also an association with *La Traviata*, the title of which is translated, in Japanese, as *The Camellia Princess*.

Dollogy

This poem makes very distinctive use of a Tohoku dialect, which we have not attempted to represent in English.

'Girl-doll' is used here for the Japanese word *oshirasama*, the name of a doll or idol made by layering pieces of silk over a stick as part of a Tohoku regional village ritual. Girls and women add fabric to the figure annually in tribute to the goddess manifest in the dolls. In some parts of Japan *oshirasama* appears as a male-female pair of dolls, or as one of a set of several dolls. The Japanese title of this poem is 'Ōshirasama-kō', meaning a theory of *oshirasama*.

Mechanimism

The Japanese title of this poem is *'Hatagami-kō'*, an original coinage denoting the theology of a god of machine-looms.

Flared Skirt

Buchi is a common name for a tabby cat, and refers to the cat's brown splotches.

A *kotatsu* is a low square-shaped Japanese style table that is used as a heater. The tabletop sits on top of a quilt, which is placed over the frame and the heater warms from underneath the table.

A *hanten* is a short padded jacket that was worn over kimono, pyjamas or other relaxed home clothes.

The Healds

A heald frame is part of a weaving loom. Technically, the frame works to separate and lift some of the warp yarns above others, thus allowing the shuttle to pass through holding the weft threads. Heald frames are rectangular and are supported by a set of thin wires called 'healds' or 'hettles'. The healds are attached to the frame vertically and the threads move through their eyeholes to weave the fabric.

The term *gentō* used by Arai is the Japanese translation of the Western term 'magic lantern' referring to the early slide projectors, first developed in the 17th Century, that directed light through small rectangular photographic image slides onto a wall or screen.

We have used 'whirlwind' to translate the Japanese word *kamaitachi*, which is a term used to describe the cutting turbulent winds common in Japan's northern snow country. Traditional folk tales tell of weasel-like creatures that fly on these whirlwinds slashing at human skin. In this poem, the focus is on the wind rather than these mythological creatures.

Banzai translates roughly as 'hurray' and literally as 'long life'. In contemporary Japan, *banzai* is used to express congratulations, although the term was most commonly used during WWII to express respect for the emperor.

Coiffeur translates the Japanese word *kamiyui*, referring to the traditional profession of a Japanese hair dresser or barber.

My Daughter's Room

The 'red draft slip' mentioned here is the draft notice that families received when their sons were drafted to war was written on red paper and so was referred to as *akagami*, literally 'red paper'.

Stone Monument

During the war, Chiran, located in Kagoshima prefecture, served as an airbase for kamikaze pilots.

We have used 'human torpedo' for the Japanese *kaiten*, which refers to the miniature submarine suicide torpedoes, manned by one sailor, that were used at the very end of WWII by the Japanese navy.

Girl 2

The Japanese term *kinrō teishin-tai* directly translates as 'Voluntary Labour Corps', however, during WWII this term was used to refer to women and girls who were drafted for sexual and industrial labour. It came to be used as a euphemism for military comfort women.

'Having been able to safeguard and maintain the structure of the Imperial State, We are always with ye, Our good and loyal subjects, relying upon your sincerity and integrity......': This is an extract from Emperor Showa's surrender speech which was broadcast at noon on the 15th of August 1945. We have used the translation quoted in Robert J.C. Butow's *Japan's Decision to Surrender*, published in 1954 by Stanford University Press.

Yakisoba

The title of the poem 'Yakisoba' in Japanese is written in the Roman alphabet and capitalised.

Yakisoba is a stir-fried noodle with sauce.

Kiriboshi daikon is dried daikon radish. *Hijiki* is a type of dried seaweed. *Katsu* curry is curry with *katsu*, which is a deep fried chicken, beef or pork with bread crumbs. 'Strawberry shortcake' is a sponge cake with strawberries and fresh cream, and 'Mont Blanc' is a little mountain shaped cake with chestnut puree.

Two quotations in this poem are idiosyncratic mixture of Japanese and English. Jeffrey Angles explains the first quotation means 'Hey lady, take a look! *Good sauce is included!*' and the second quotation means 'Wow, this is *rather cheap*, isn't it?' (*Poems of Hiromi Itō, Toshiko Hirata & Takako Arai*, Vagabond Press, 2016, pp.129-130).

Iie is paired with *arigatō* (thank you), meaning 'no worries' or 'that's ok'.

Eels and Catfish

Junsai are young lotus stems.

The Seventh of the Twenty-Fourth Month

In Japanese the word *michiyuki* means both a simple journey and the suicidal journey to death taken by star-crossed lovers, so often portrayed in *jōruri* and *kabuki* theatre. Hirata plays with the layered meaning of this word, using it as both a boy's name and just such a suicidal journey.

Welcome Home

The original title is '*Okaeri*', meaning 'welcome home'. This, paired with *tadaima*, is a very common household greeting exchange. A returning family member will say '*tadaima*', meaning 'I'm arriving just now', as soon as they open the front door, and whoever is in the house welcomes the person with '*okaeri*'.

This poem uses *katakana* script for words which usually do not appear in *katakana*, which draws visual attention.

The Fruit of Summer Drips Like Blood

Obama is the city in Fukui prefecture where the poet was born and grew up.

Sōmen is a skinny udon-like noodle, usually eaten cold with a dipping sauce in summer.

This poem is taken from a poetry collection called *Tiger is Here* (2015). The image of the beast or tiger that's included in this poem is used throughout the collection.

Proposals for New Forms of Alternative Energy: Spin Cycle, Shoe Power

Both of these poems are taken from a poetry sequence with 41 parts called '*Daitai enerugii suishin demo*' ('A March for Alternative Energy'), written for theatrical performance.

'Shoe Power' contains references to the very famous poem *'Ame nimo makezu'* ('Strong in the Rain') written by Miyazawa Kenji (1896-1933). The phrases 'strong in the rain', 'strong in the wind' quote this poem, as does the phrase which we translate as 'I want to be *all that'*.

Into White Darkness

This poem was first published in an anthology of poems on the 2011 earthquake/tsunami disaster in Tohoku, Japan, *Rōsokuno honoo ga sasayaku kotoba* (*Words whispered by the candle light*, 2011).

The Gold Fish

The Japanese title of this poem, *'Ryūkin'*, is the name of a specific type of goldfish. These are originally from Okinawa (The kingdom of Ryūkyū) and have a long fluttering tail.

The Gift

Some parts of this poem use a Western Japanese dialect, which we have not attempted to represent in English.

Washing Machine, The Market

These poems are both taken from the poetry collection, *Yoihikari* (*Good Light*, 2016), which records the poet's month-long stay in Berlin.

And the Bright Morning Comes

This poem won a prize in Iwate prefecture's Disaster Poetry Competition, and was published in the *Shishū, Iwate shinsai siika 2017* (*Iwate Disaster Poetry Anthology, 2017*).

● : This character makes a coded reference to the government. During WWII, painted black marks were used to censor texts, and some literary works were almost entirely covered with black. This black dot covers a one-word Japanese character, making the reference clearer for some readers.

Some phrases in the poem's prose sections are taken from public signage.

The phrase 'only plastic bags' references the use of bags to hold dry ice to help preserve bodies following death.

In Buddhist tradition, the 49th day (called *Shijūku-nichi* in Japanese), marks the point at which the spirit of a dead person can be reborn. Accordingly, bereaved families commemorate this day as a moment of further parting.

Coming Home for a Brief Visit

Bon-matsuri is a traditional village festival, held all over Japan, in *bon* season (around August 15th). It is a season in which the souls of the dead return home, and each household welcomes their return. At *bon-matsuri,* villagers come together for a circle dance ritual.

BIOGRAPHIES

Listed using the Japanese convention of family name followed by a given name.

Japanese Poets

ARAI, TAKAKO

Arai Takako was born in 1966 in Kiryū City, Gunma prefecture, Japan to a family engaged in textile manufacturing, a traditional industry in the region. Her first collection of poetry, *Hao-bekki*, was published in 1997. Since 1998 she has been a regular contributor to, and eventually editor of *Mi'Te*, a journal featuring poetry and criticism (http://www.mi-te-press.net/). Her second collection, *Tamashii Dansu* (2007) was awarded the 41st Oguma Hideo Poetry Prize, and several of the works from the collection have been translated in *Soul Dance: Poems by Takako Arai* (Mi'Te Press, 2008, tr. Jeffrey Angles). Two of the poems included here are from her third collection, *Betto to Shokki (Beds and Looms*, 2013). Since 2014, she has been deeply involved with a regional language poetry project in Ōfunato city in Iwate prefecture, which was severely damaged by the Tohoku Earthquake and Tsunami in 2011. Two of the poems here, 'A Lightbulb' and 'Dollogy' emerge from this project and are as yet uncollected in Arai's books.

ISHIKAWA, ITSUKO

Ishikawa Itsuko (b.1933) is a committed anti-war and anti-nuclear activist poet. She was born in Tokyo, and was 12 years old when WWII ended. The war experiences of her childhood left her with a legacy of perceiving her naive culpability in the violence of Japanese Imperial Army across Asia and the Pacific. She has written extensively in both poetry and prose on the topic, particularly on Japanese government authoritarianism and the victimisation of women in war. The poem 'Wolf' included here is the title poem of her second collection, which was awarded Mr H Prize (1961). 'Stone Monument' was published in her 1985 collection, *Chidorigafuchi e ikimashita ka (Have You Been to Chidorigafuchi?)*, which won the 11th Earth Prize.

ITO, HIROMI

Ito Hiromi, born in Tokyo in 1955, is a celebrated poet who has won many awards. She quickly became a leading figure in women's poetry in Japan on the publication of her first poetry collection in 1978. She has published not only poems but essays on motherhood and child-rearing, which became a new literary genre for Japanese women writers. A prolific writer, her poetry and prose on women's lives have been published in *Onna no zetsubō (The Despair of Women,* 2008), *Heikei-ki (The Book of Menopause,* 2013) and *Onna no issyō (A Life of a Woman,* 2014). Her works on life and death include *Inu gokoro (Dog Heart,* 2013), *Chichi no ikiru (Father Lives,* 2014), *Kodama kusadama (Tree Spirits Glass Spirits,* 2014) and *Seppuku-kō (Thoughts on Harakiri,* 2017). In her two latest poetry collections, *Kawara arekusa (Wild Glass on the Riverbank,* 2005, tr. Jeffrey Angles) and *Togenuki shin sugamo jizō engi (New Tales of Sugamo Pilgrimage,* 2007), she has created a unique poetic narrative form inspired by early moralistic story telling in Buddhist teachings. Her interest in Buddhism has led her to trans-create some early Buddhist texts into contemporary Japanese.

KAWAGUCHI, HARUMI

Kawaguchi Harumi was born in Obama, Fukui prefecture, Japan in 1962. While attending Waseda University, Tokyo, she started writing poems and published her first collection, *Mizuhime* (*Water Princess*, 1985) on graduation. She worked for more than seven years for one of the biggest trading companies in Japan, has taught creative writing courses at various universities, and edited several anthologies. Her tenth poetry collection, *Map of the Peninsula* (2009), received the 10th Yamamoto Kenkichi Literary Prize, and her latest collection, *Tiger is Here* (2015) won the 46th Takami Jun Poetry Prize. Three of her poems included here are from *Map of the Peninsula*, and two are from *Tiger is Here*.

KONO, SATOKO

Born in Fukuoka prefecture, Japan, in 1972. All three of her poems included in this anthology are from her fifth poetry collection, *Chijō de okita dekigoto wa zenbu kokokara miteiru* (*Everything Happening on Earth has been Watched from Here*, 2017). This collection is visually innovative, published on black paper with white lettering and avant-garde design. She leads a group of young artists, TOLTA, which she describes as a 'verbal art unit', and which challenges the boundaries of poetry through performance, installation and graphic text work. She edited the anthology *Centenary of Japanese Contemporary Poetry* (2015) and writes monthly book reviews for *Western Japan Newspaper*.

HIRATA, TOSHIKO

Hirata Toshiko (b. 1955) is one of Japan's most celebrated contemporary poets. She is well known not only for poetry, but also for plays, short stories, novellas and essays. Her poetry, prose and plays have won multiple awards, including the Shichōsha New Poet's Award (1983), the Bansui Poetry Award (1998), the Theatrical Creative Award (2000), the Noma Literary New Writer's Prize (2005), and the Murasaki-shikibu Literary Prize (2016). The poems included in this anthology are collected in *Shinanoka* (*Is it Poetry? A Poem on the Seventh Day*), which was awarded the Hagiwara Sagkutarō Prize (2004). For *Shinanoka*, more information can be found at: http://www.biwako. shiga-u.ac.jp/eml/WP/No228.pdf.

MISAKI, TAKAKO

Misaki Takako was born in Chiba prefecture, Japan, in 1967. She started writing in her late teens, attending a poetry writing class taught by Yoshihara Sachiko (1932-2002), a feminist poet who ran a famous feminist poetry journal, *La Mer*, and encouraged other women to write. In 1990, Misaki was awarded the 7th La Mer New Poet's Award, and published her first collection, *Kannō kensashitsu* (*Sensual Examination Room*, 1991). After graduating Ochanomizu University, she worked in a bank for six years, got married and became a mother, entering an 11-year silence between her second (1995) and third (2006) poetry collections. Her third collection, *Sakura byōin shūhen* (*Around Sakura Hospital*), won the prestigious Takami Jun Poetry Prize, which drew her back to the world of poetry. Her fourth collection, *Shizukani, kowareteiru niwa* (*Silently Decaying Garden*, 2011) was awarded the Ono-city Poetry Prize. Her poems have been anthologised and 'Into White Darkness', collected in this anthology, has been printed in Japanese school textbooks.

MISUMI, MIZUKI

Misumi Mizuki is an award-winning poet who was born in 1981, in Kagoshima prefecture, Japan. Her poems were first published in poetry journals while she was studying art and design at Tokyo Zokei University. In 2004, at the age of 22, she received the 42th Gendaishi-techō Poetry Prize. Her first poetry collection, *Overkill* (2004) was awarded the Nakahara Chūya Poetry Prize. Her second collection won both the Rekitei New Writer's Award and the South Japan Literary Prize in 2006. Her fifth collection received the Hagiwara Sakutarō Prize in 2014, the youngest poet ever to receive this prestigious prize. She is an active poetry performer, both within and outside Japan.

NAKAMURA, SACHIKO

Nakamura Sachiko was born in 1963, in Ōfunato-city, Iwate prefecture. Born to a landlord family who had lived there for hundreds of years, she has never left her home town, which became one of the areas severely damaged by the 2011 Tohoku earthquake and tsunami. Although she has yet to publish a collection in Japan's tightly controlled poetry book scene, Nakamura has established a striking body of poems that have won individual recognition through local competitions and newspaper publication. 'And the Bright Morning Comes' is one such poem, having won the Iwate Disaster Poetry Prize, as well as being anthologised and broadcast on radio in commemoration of the Tohoku earthquake disaster.

YAMASAKI, KAYOKO

Yamasaki Kayoko is a Japanese-Serbian poet and translator, who was born in 1956 and has been living in Belgrade since 1981. She is the author of twelve poetry books (six in Japanese and six in Serbian). Her works have received literary awards including the Yomiuri Award (for *A Poetry Diary from Belgrade*, 2015) and the Milica Stojadinovic Award (for *Flowers in Water*, 2015). She performs poetry at refugee camps and schools, and is a professor at Belgrade University.

Translators

ANGLES, JEFFREY

Jeffrey Angles, born in 1971, is a poet, translator, and professor of Japanese literature at Western Michigan University in Kalamazoo (USA). His collection of original Japanese-language poetry *Watashi no hizukehenkōsen* (*My International Date Line*, 2016) won the highly coveted Yomiuri Prize for Literature, an honour accorded to only a few non-native speakers since the award began in 1949. Among his numerous book-length translations are *Forest of Eyes: Selected Poems of Tada Chimako* (University of California Press), *Killing Kanoko: Selected Poems of Itō Hiromi* (Action Books), *Wild Grass on the Riverbank* by Itō Hiromi (Action Books), and *Twelve Views from the Distance* by Takahashi Mutsuo (University of Minnesota Press). His translation of Tada Chimako won both the Japan-US Friendship Commission Prize for the Translation of Japanese Literature and the Landon Translation Prize from the American Academy of Poets.

ATHERTON, CASSANDRA

Cassandra Atherton is an award-winning prose poet, scholar and critic. She was a Visiting Professor at the Institute of Comparative Culture at Sophia University, Tokyo in 2014 and a Visiting Scholar at Harvard University in 2016. She has published eight books and over the last three years has been invited to edit six special editions of leading refereed journals. She was recently awarded an Australia Council Grant to write a book of prose poetry on the Hiroshima Maidens.

CRAWFORD, JEN

Jen Crawford's recent poetry publications include *Koel* (Cordite Books) and the chapbook *lichen loves stone* (Tinfish Press). She teaches poetry and creative writing within the Centre for Creative and Cultural Research at the University of Canberra, and has also taught in Singapore and Aotearoa/New Zealand. She grew up in Aotearoa/New Zealand and the Philippines and holds a PhD from the University of Wollongong.

FANAIYAN, NILOOFAR

Niloofar Fanaiyan is a writer and poet currently based in Haifa, Israel. She was the 2016 Donald Horne Research Fellow at the Centre for Creative and Cultural Research, University of Canberra, where she obtained her PhD. She received the Canberra Critics Circle Literary Award for Poetry for her book of poems titled *Transit* (RWP, 2016).

HAYES, CAROL

Dr Carol Hayes is the Associate Dean of Student Experience at the ANU College of Asia and the Pacific. She is a senior lecturer in Japanese language and literature and teaches both Japanese language and courses about Japan in English ranging from literature, to culture and film. Her primary research focuses on modern and contemporary Japanese literature and cultural studies. Past work has focused on Hagiwara Sakutarō and other modern poets, the portrayals of the Pacific War in Japanese film and zainichi cultural identity in literature. Recent poetry translations co-authored with Rina Kikuchi have appeared in the 2015 edition of *Poetry Kanto* and the recent issues of *Transference*.

JAIRETH, SUBHASH

Subhash Jaireth, now Canberra based, was born in Khanna and spent nine years in Moscow between 1969 and 1978 before returning to India. He has published three collections of poetry and four books of fiction and non-fiction in Hindi, Russian and English. His book of poetic prose pieces *Incantations* (Recent Work Press) was released in September 2016.

KIKUCHI, RINA

Rina Kikuchi is an associate professor at Shiga University, Japan. She has an M.A. in comparative literary theories from the University of Warwick, UK, and a Ph.D in contemporary Irish poetry from Chiba University, for which her study included a year of research at Trinity College, Dublin. At present, she is a visiting fellow at ANU and the University of Canberra, and conducting her research on modern and contemporary Japanese women's poetry, which includes translating their works into English.

MUNDEN, PAUL

Paul Munden is a Postdoctoral Research Fellow at the University of Canberra, where he is also Program Manager for the International Poetry Studies Institute. He has published four collections of poetry, including *The Bulmer Murder* (Recent Work Press, 2017), and a new collection, *Chromatic*, will be published by UWAP in October.

SMITH, MELINDA

Melinda Smith is the author of five poetry books, the most recent of which is *Goodbye, Cruel* (Pitt St Poetry, 2017). Her work has been anthologised widely and translated into multiple languages. She received the 2014 Prime Minister's Literary Award for poetry. She is based in the ACT and is a former poetry editor of for the *Canberra Times*.

STRANGE, SHANE

Shane Strange tutors and lectures in Writing and Literary Studies at the University of Canberra. He is a writer whose poetry and short form writing has been published widely in Australia. He is also a publisher and editor at Recent Work Press, a small press based in Canberra, Australia.

Acknowledgements

FOR THE POEMS IN JAPANESE

「電球」（『ミて』132号2015年秋）、「おーしらさま考」（『ミて』134号2016年春）、「機神考」（『現代詩100周年』2015年）、「フレアスカート」及び「ヘルド」（『ベットと織機』2013年）、「狼・私たち」（『狼・私たち』1960年）、「ヒラメのこと」（『子どもと戦争』1976年）、「娘の部屋」及び「石の碑」（『千鳥ケ淵へ行きましたか』1985年）、「少女2」（『砕かれた花たちへのレクイエム』1994年）、「父の子宮あるいは一枚の地図」（『のろとさにわ』1991年）、「鰻と鯰」及び「YAKISOBA」（『現代詩手帖』「日系人の現在　小詩集」2011年9月号）、「一月七日」「十三月七日」及び「二十四月七日」（『詩七日』2004年）、「半島の地図」「席」及び「おかえり」（『半島の地図』2009年）、「人造」及び「夏の果は血のように滴る」（『Tiger is here.』2015年）、「専用」「エアロバイク洗濯マシーン」及び「靴」（『地上で起きた出来事はぜんぶここからみている』2017年）、「白い闇のほうへ」及び「琉金」（『飛びたたせなかったほうの蝶々』2015年）、「プレゼント」（『カナシヤル』2006年）、「洗濯機」及び「市場」（『よいひかり』2016年）、「まぶしい朝が来て」（『いわて震災詩歌2017』2017年）、「砂時計」及び「木」（『鳥のために』1995年）、「一時帰国」（『みをはやみ』2010年）

FOR TRANSLATIONS IN ENGLISH

'A Lightbulb', 'Dollogy' and 'Mechanimism' (*Cordite Poetry Review,* issue 82 August 2017); 'Flared Skirt' and 'The Healds' (*Transference,* volume 3 Fall 2015); 'My Daughter's Room', 'Stone Monument' and 'Girl 2' (*Transference,* volume 4 Fall 2016); 'My Father's Uterus, or the Map', 'Yakisoba' and 'Eels and Catfish' *(Poems of Hiromi Itō Toshiko Hirata & Takako Arai,* tr. by Jeffrey Angles. Vagabond Press, Asia Pacific Poetry Series, 2016); 'The Seventh of the First Month', 'The Seventh of the Thirteenth Month' and 'The Seventh of the Twenty-Fourth Month' *(Poetry Kanto,* No.31 2015).